The NEW EXECUTIVE ASSISTANT

The NEW EXECUTIVE ASSISTANT

Exceptional executive office management

Jonathan McIlroy

MONTEREY
PRESS

First Published in 2018
by Monterey Press
7 Westbourne St
Brunswick VIC 3056
Australia
www.montereypress.com

Cover artwork by Mihail Uvarov
Designed and typeset by Lu Sexton

National Library of Australia

A catalogue record for this
book is available from the
National Library of Australia

ISBN: 9780648116301 (paperback)

This book is dedicated to the many long-suffering executive assistants (EAs) of the world, working for dinosaurs in prehistoric organisations, who have dreamed of being able to have a more fulfilled career. It is also dedicated to all those fabulous EAs and executives who have already created, or are in the process of creating, better working practices and ways of supporting each other. They work in true partnerships, and I have been incredibly privileged to get to know many of them over the years.

Acknowledgments

I would like to acknowledge all the wonderful people who made the production of this book possible and assisted me at different stages.

In particular I would like to thank my twin sons, Callum and Connor, and my partner, Paula, for their support and patience throughout the process and for their feedback – and often frank opinions – on so many elements of the book, from content to design.

Many thanks are due to my business partner, Natasha Canon, who co-founded Executive Assistant Network and has worked alongside me on its direction, growth and continued evolution through Australia and, more recently, globally. Thanks too to all the staff at EAN, both present and past, who provided thoughts and ideas as I created many of the models, frameworks and elements of our training and education programs, which have ultimately found their way into this book.

I would also like to acknowledge the many thousands of EAs who have shared ideas with me over the years and who have contributed at conferences or in surveys, and the many incredible executives who have also shared their ideas and thoughts at our conferences or in private discussions. Without their collective stories I would never have been able to conceptualise the vision for the EA-Executive Partnership Model contained in this book, or to intellectualise and create business frameworks and models to evolve that vision in practical ways. I hope this will ultimately lead to better ways of working for EAs and their executives in many thousands of different organisations.

Finally, I would like to give special mention to the EAs and executives who contributed directly to the book and have their contributions included in the Appendix. I sought their thoughts, opinions and ideas to validate the assertions and vision contained within each chapter and I believe they succeed in doing just that. So my sincere thanks to them.

Contents

Introduction

The New Executive Assistant is a guide for both EAs and their executives, designed to help both parties get more from the way they work together. However, rather than a prescriptive and exhaustive tome, full of set rules and ideas, it is designed to be more of a handbook, introducing frameworks and models that will help EAs and their executives find their own best ways of working together.

That is not to say that I have shied away from making some strong recommendations. I have some fairly strong opinions on certain aspects of EA-executive partnerships and I share these – particular with respect to outdated position descriptions and outdated executive perceptions about what they want from their EAs.

The original *raison d'être* for the role of the EA was to provide basic clerical and administrative support to assist the executive function, which included saving executives from having to perform menial tasks themselves.

Today the role is potentially much more sophisticated, as this book goes to some lengths to explain. A really good *new* EA manages the office of their executive in a way that enables the executive to be at their most productive and effective. The EA enhances executive productivity in numerous ways, many of which are rarely seen or understood – though hopefully these less obvious areas of assistance will be clearer once you've read this book. Today's EAs should no longer be purely reactive, waiting to be directed by their boss. Rather they should be proactive, playing a management role themselves – a role that is so much more than just minding the day-to-day functioning of the executive office. Today's EA plays a partnership role in managing their executive's time, energy, focus, mindset, priorities and relationships.

Great EAs are facilitators of the best outcomes for the whole executive team, including all their managerial and other team members. They are not the intransigent 'gatekeepers' of yesteryear, those who used proximity to power to wield power of their own. Rather they rely on relationship building, persuasion and building trust with people throughout the organisation in order that they can do those things that are in the best interests of the executive and the rest of the team at any time.

But there is a lot of nuance to all this, which is where I go into depth in this book. There are plenty of intangible elements to the role that rarely make it into any EA position descriptions, and I aim to uncover these, to make them clearer and, via models and frameworks, provide guidance to both EAs and executives as they seek to make every element of the EA role work to the benefit of everyone.

Something I draw on a few times in *The New Executive Assistant* is the notion of spectrums or continuums. There are so many aspects of the EA-executive partnership in which there is no one 'right' answer – in which each pair of EA and executive needs to find their own way of working from along a spectrum of possibilities. While this means, of course, that there is no definitive right way for EAs and their executives to work together overall, I do argue that there are definitely some very wrong, outdated ways of working. While these approaches, described early in the book, have clearly had their time, they are still surprisingly common, despite the fact that they negatively affect executive performance and productivity, and hinder organisational output.

As well as providing models and frameworks, this book highlights exactly what skills and knowledge areas EAs should seek to enhance and why, all designed to help them be more proactive and able to take on more for their executive so the executive can focus on their key priorities at any time.

Something else I'm aiming to achieve with this book is to help executives and their organisations avoid a number of mistakes my colleagues and I have observed frequently in recent years. These include poorly thought through rationalisation and offshoring of support services. We know that the vast majority of those who undertake such projects live to rue the day. And we know why. It always has to do with underestimating the real contribution made by EAs, with executives and their teams suffering a loss of productivity as a result. It's a classic case of 'you don't know what you've got 'til it's gone'.

It still astounds me how poorly understood the benefits of a good EA are. Too many executives assume that their company's ridiculously outdated position descriptions for executive assistants actually define what those assistants are capable of, yet the PDs nearly always fall well short. Poorly prepared PDs exist in the vast majority of organisations we work with.

At its core this book is a guide to help EAs, their executives and their organisations reconsider the role, the relationships and EA-executive partnerships in more structured and focussed ways. My premise is that the more effective the EA, the more effective the executive ... and the more effective the organisation.

The New Executive Assistant provides EAs and executives with the tools they both need to ensure they get the best out of themselves and each other by maximising the effectiveness of every EA-executive partnership. Use the frameworks, models and lists presented as a handbook for building trust, strengthening EA capability and broadening the scope of the EA role. I guarantee every single EA and executive pairing will find information here that will help them achieve better outcomes as they work together.

1

From secretary to PA to EA

The evolution of the role of
the executive assistant

BACK IN THE 1950S AND '60S, when real-life Don Drapers roamed the offices of the planet, the role of the secretary, as she (it was always a 'she') was called, was cut and dried. She would answer the phone for her boss, type up letters and manage his diary. For the most part her duties were routine and low-tech, reactive and directed. Her perspective was essentially local, bound by the four walls of the office. Her ability to show initiative was limited to perhaps reminding her boss of his wife's birthday.

Things have changed … or at least they should have.

The new executive assistant (EA) works *in partnership* with their executive. They are proactive and managing. Far more than the secretary of the '50s, or even the personal assistant of the '90s, the new EA manages the office in a way that enables the executive to be as effective and productive as possible. They work alongside their executive but also unilaterally, anticipating the latter's needs while managing his or her priorities in line with shared and understood goals and objectives. The new EA has a much broader perspective than their predecessors, and so has the potential to better comprehend the relative importance of constantly shifting priorities.

This book is a guide for executives and their assistants who find themselves working somewhere in the space between the secretary of the 1950s and the new executive assistant of the 2010s. You may have moved beyond the *Mad Men* era – that was a long time ago now – but perhaps you haven't quite reached the level of partnership that is possible. As an executive, you may still be seeing your assistant primarily as a way of handing off administrative support to someone whose hourly cost to the organisation is much lower than yours; as an EA your work may be defined by a position description that hasn't changed substantially for 30 years or more.

The New Executive Assistant is a manual for executives who are open to learning how they can dramatically improve their productivity and performance – not by eking out small improvements in their own personal productivity (perhaps spending large amounts on high-priced coaches, retreats and/or technologies in order to do so), but by achieving significantly larger – potentially double-digit – gains by working more effectively in partnership with their assistant.

For assistants, this book aims to show them exactly how they can provide more productive and effective assistance. It points to areas where assistants could be supporting their executive but, in my experience and that of my colleagues, probably are not doing so – areas of new responsibility for the new EA. It will help assistants to identify ways of working more independently, despite the constantly shifting priorities of their executives and organisations in the 21st-century office.

The New Executive Assistant will help executives and their assistants together assess their pairings and how these partnerships can thrive, growing stronger, more effective and more productive through a clearer mutual understanding of the many tangible and intangible benefits EAs can bring to their workplaces.

Finally, this book should serve as a note of caution to those businesses considering the rationalisation of their executive assistant roles. This, unfortunately, is something I have witnessed more and more often in recent years, usually in the misguided belief that technology can replace the role of the EA and reduce costs at the same time. More often than not, these executives realise too late that they acted in haste and that technology simply cannot replace the real, if often intangible, benefits that an EA can bring to both their executive and the wider organisation.

From the past to the future

Let's explore the evolution of the executive assistant's role a little more. For a long time the secretary/PA was someone who was given tasks to perform by their executive – tasks that saved the executive time and effort. Doing the job effectively required a certain skillset, including typing, shorthand and minute taking – skills that the executive didn't typically share. Nevertheless, the role wasn't valued much beyond the tasks and duties the assistant performed.

For these traditional roles, position descriptions – where they existed – were very task focussed (see Figure 1). From managing diary appointments to booking travel to handling correspondence, the assistant's tasks were very simple, with outcomes that were self-evident and easy to assess. They either did or didn't do what they were asked; they did or didn't achieve the simple outcomes required. There was no need for KPIs linked to business goals because the assistant wasn't seen as having a direct impact on the business.

It should be obvious to anyone who acts in either an executive role or an EA role that the latter has changed dramatically.

First and foremost, as mentioned earlier, the new EA is proactive and managing, not reactive and directed. The job sits alongside rather than 'under' the executive, operating largely in a management capacity. The goal isn't to simply reduce the executive's workload, but rather to find ways to improve their effectiveness by managing their office.

Second, the perspective of the new EA is much broader than it was. It is something of a cliché to talk about executives needing a helicopter or birds-eye view of their organisation, but there is a lot of truth in the idea. The new EA will both share large parts of that view and contribute towards the formation of it, drawing on a working knowledge and understanding of the strategic objectives of the organisation and the executive, and of the many projects being pursued to help achieve those objectives.

Third, the new EA plays a prominent, if not the pre-eminent, role in assessing and managing their executive's priorities. By having a clearer view of the goals and objectives of their own role, those of their executive and those of the organisation as a whole, today's assistant is capable of assessing shifting priorities and making decisions on behalf of their executive, often without direct reference to them.

Purpose of the Position

The purpose of the position is to provide high level administrative, clerical and organisational support to the Chief Executive Officer.

Executive Assistant duties and responsibilities

The EA is responsible for ensuring the smooth, efficient and timely running of the office.

- Organise and manage the CEO's office and electronic and paper files.
- Manage the meeting schedule and calendar for the CEO, including scheduling and organising all internal and external meetings.
- Coordinate and book travel and accommodation for the CEO and maintain detailed travel itineraries.
- Assist the CEO with the preparation of presentations, papers and reports as required.
- Assist in the preparation of agendas and minutes for board meetings and gather all the reports and information necessary from all contributors to board papers.
- Support the CEO with the management of electronic and paper communications as required including drafting emails and letters as required.
- Organise and coordinate events, functions, meetings, training and restaurant bookings.
- Maintain all stationery and other supplies required by the CEO and their office.
- Meet and welcome visitors and guests of the CEO.

Executive Assistant job qualifications and requirements

The EA must be professional in both nature and appearance as the first point of contact for many people with the CEO, their office and the broader organisation.

In addition, the EA must have:

- highly developed written communication skills with strong attention to detail
- effective verbal communication and interpersonal skills
- strong time management and prioritisation skills
- sound knowledge of administrative systems, technologies and procedures
- skills in the use of Microsoft Office products, particularly Outlook, Word, Excel and PowerPoint.

Figure 1: A traditional EA position description

Beyond all this, the role of the new EA also includes more responsibilities specific to their role in managing the office of the executive, and in doing so ensures the executive is their most productive and effective. This involves the EA being involved in helping to manage more than just the executive's priorities, but also their energy, focus, mindset and relationships while, of course, also facilitating and managing the timely and relevant flow of information to the executive, as well as access to them.

Unfortunately, while the role of the EA may have changed, understanding of the role, particularly among those who do not have an assistant, has not. Misconceptions about the role of the EA or PA and the benefits it brings are rife in both business and non-business circles. Hollywood certainly hasn't helped here. The TV series *Mad Men* clearly showed the role as it was decades ago: very directed, open to sexist abuse, and more about serving the master than working alongside him. Perhaps the character of Donna in another TV series, *Suits*, comes closest to showing the potential of the role when someone with broad knowledge and skills, along with great strength of character, is in the role, though our experience is that great EAs in real life are more strategic and much less showy in going about the business of doing their jobs.

These misconceptions are important to understand, because they help explain the difficulty that exists in trying to professionalise a role that has evolved with no real structure or guidance, and that varies from one EA and executive pairing to the next as much as it varies from one organisation to the next.

We have come to differentiate the role of the new EA in terms of its 'tangible' and 'intangible' elements, the tangible elements being those more traditional functions and tasks, and the intangible elements being all the additional work that is of high value but can be hard to pin down.

I will examine each of these in more detail throughout the book, and in Chapter 11 I provide guidance on modernising EA position descriptions and performance measurement.

EA value – executive, business and EA benefits

Understanding, let alone quantifying, the true value of an executive assistant and the extent to which they improve executive productivity and effectiveness is exceptionally difficult.

One of the reasons why EA position descriptions often continue to focus on documenting the same simple tasks that have been common to assistants for many years is that those are the tasks that are easy to identify. However, so much of what the new EA does for their executive and organisation is neither noted nor widely understood. This makes describing the EA job in detail quite difficult, which in turn means measuring their true performance is almost impossible.

But if this is true, how can we reconcile the notion of an EA being 'invaluable', as we so often hear executives say? Why is it that we continue to hear comments – partly in jest and to some extent patronising – like, 'We all know where the real power lies', or 'We know who wields the power behind the throne' or even 'We know who really runs the organisation'? Why have so many successful business tycoons included in their autobiographies references to their EAs, stating something along the lines of, 'I couldn't have done it without my assistant'? Why do most executives dread their assistant going away on leave?

While most executives inherently understand the value of their EA, most have spent very little time trying to quantify that value or fully understand the benefits delivered by them. With only outdated position descriptions to fall back on, many tangible and intangible areas of EA responsibility are taken for granted.

Executives know their EA is valuable, but they have no idea how to measure that value.

When I speak to EAs about this, most confirm that their annual reviews are almost entirely subjective. Some have limited KPIs aligned with the tasks of their position descriptions, but in most cases their appraisal comes down to how well they get along with the executive and the rapport they share. Now obviously the level of rapport is a strong indicator of how well they are working together, and it shouldn't be discounted, but it isn't formal enough to help assess how things could be improved – and certainly is unlikely to be understood in terms of the vast benefits the EA is delivering that go unnoticed.

In a series of polls conducted across Australia in 2016 by our training organisation, Executive Assistant Academy, we learned that only around 20 per cent of EAs believed they had a position description that accurately reflected their role. Only around 5 per cent believed they had a meaningful performance assessment process that truly reflected the value they deliver to their organisations!

If it is so hard for executives to articulate the real value of their EA, despite working alongside them every day, imagine how hard it is for others in an organisation to do so, such as those in human resources or finance.

Misguided rationalisation

Lack of understanding of an EA's true value has its most detrimental impact when it comes to role rationalisation. In recent years we have seen many organisations go through rationalisations or restructures in which they have dismissed large percentages of their EA or PA workforce.

Decisions to strip back the number of assistants are often based on assessments of their roles and responsibilities as indicated by their (outdated – see Figure 1) position descriptions rather than on genuine assessments of their true value. In one global business services firm I heard about, a process not dissimilar to a 'time and motion' study was undertaken to try and assess where assistants were spending their time, as a precursor to a rationalisation process.

A common scenario is one in which the ratio of assistants to executives shifts from one assistant to one executive to one to three or even more, with perhaps only the very top echelon of executives maintaining a dedicated EA. In other cases, EA roles are rationalised on the basis of tasks, with one group of assistants focussing on travel management, for instance, while another focusses on event management.

My experience is that these rationalisations have tended to fail miserably. As should be apparent by now, the new EA performs so much more than routine, tangible tasks like booking airline tickets or caterers. When their role is reduced to no more than these and other administrative responsibilities, a large number of intangible tasks – all the strategic, 'big picture', anticipatory stuff that I described earlier – are no longer performed. Crude assessments of the EA's role fail because they overlook their new, larger role and the value of that role.

A model for the new EA – why it's necessary and what it delivers

All the issues discussed so far – essentially the misunderstanding and undervaluing of the new EA role – are what prompted our organisation to devise a model (Figure 2) – the EA-Executive Partnership Model – to assist with improving understanding of the new EA role, particularly with respect to the intangible aspects of the role. The model focusses on areas of responsibility that are not widely understood, rather than simply restating those routine tasks that appear in traditional job descriptions for assistants.

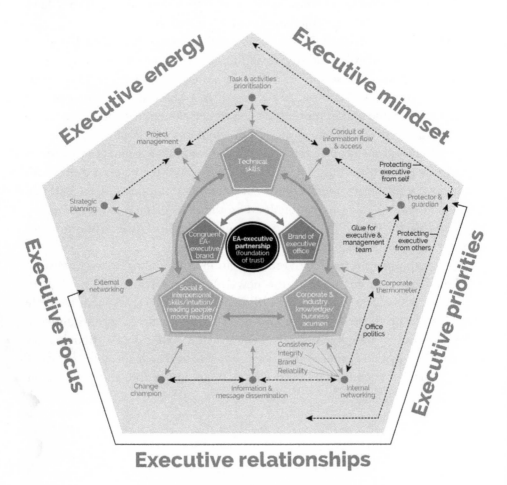

Figure 2: The EA-Executive Partnership Model
(Larger version available at www.executiveassistant.com/partnershipmodel)

In the remainder of this book we are going to examine the role of the new EA based on these areas of responsibility, the interplay between them and their impact on executive energy, focus, mindset, priorities and relationships. Areas to be covered include:

- a model for building trust between EA and executive that can remove the reliance on this only evolving slowly and organically over time

- focussing on how a 'brand' for the office of the executive can evolve when a true partnership is established, and when the brand of the EA and executive are congruent and aligned

- understanding all the technical skills, business acumen, corporate and industry knowledge, and social and interpersonal skills EAs need to succeed

- the EA's role in managing current and shifting priorities and their relative importance, based on a sound knowledge and clear understanding of strategic objectives and current projects

- the EA as a conduit to facilitate the flow of information and access to the executive based on a knowledge of the relative importance of different priorities

- the EA's role in protecting the executive from others, knowing when to act as a facilitator and conduit to ensure projects and initiatives can be delivered, while also knowing when to act as a gatekeeper to help manage executive focus, energy and mindset; why this is essential to ensuring that the executive maintains peak performance and peak mental flow without undue interruption

- the EA staying attuned to those times when they need to act to protect the executive from themselves if they are to effectively manage their energy, mindset and focus – and even their wellbeing – and maintain their optimal performance level

- the EA as corporate thermometer for the executive, judiciously filtering chatter and noise to keep the executive abreast of what is happening throughout the team, division and wider organisation, all the time being aware of when people are trying to manipulate or use the EA to achieve certain outcomes after passing on specific information

- the need for the EA to manage the interplay and relationships between the executive and direct reports – as well as between those direct reports – and acting as the glue for the team when necessary

- the EA building strategic relationships throughout the organisation that can facilitate the implementation and delivery of desired projects and initiatives

- the EA helping to disseminate information regarding initiatives, projects or policies throughout the organisation

- the EA as an ambassador and even change champion for initiatives or policies throughout the organisation at all levels, especially with key internal business network contacts

- the EA networking strategically externally to develop relationships that can facilitate the achievement of organisational or executive goals and objectives.

Important concepts

There are three important concepts that I want to explain before we get into the detail of our model. Each of these is a fundamental part of the new EA's overall role, and each has a degree of nuance that needs to be understood.

Manager of the executive office

For the new EA to reach a stage where they can effectively manage their executive's priorities, focus, energy, mindset and relationships, their role needs to be promoted to the wider organisation, and even to external connections, as manager of the executive office – with the authority that that implies. Success here depends on the development of the EA's leadership and management capabilities.

Managerial perspective and action, not to mention leadership vision and capabilities, are essential for an EA, who has to navigate competing requests for information, for access, for deliverables, while at the same time ensuring that their executive is able to maintain their focus on what they are doing and needing to achieve.

The nuance in this arrangement is that the executive needs to be seen to empower their EA to manage these areas, and they need to understand the importance of not undermining the EA's efforts on their behalf – particularly with their own direct reports. For many executives this is a difficult rule to stick to, but it is critical if the credibility of the EA as manager of the executive's office is to be preserved. Later in the book we will look at how the executive and EA working together can learn how to assess situations in a uniform way, so the executive never feels the need to act unilaterally – bypassing their EA – and vice versa.

In today's world where activity-based workplaces and other non-traditional working arrangements are becoming more common, where flatter management structures are blurring hierarchical boundaries and where executives want to be seen to be accessible, including managing their own communications and diaries in the case of the technically savvy, the ability of the EA to effectively support their executive and manage their office can sometimes be difficult. This is why it is important for the executive to give their EA the authority they need – and consistently recognise that authority – to draw on their leadership and management capabilities. Only then can the EA fully assist their executive to work effectively and efficiently, spending as much time in a state of peak mental flow as possible.

Working unilaterally where possible

The modern organisation is full of noise, and not just of the type we can hear. Organisations are highly complex and, for the executive, this complexity generates a never-ending stream of mundane interruptions and irritations that can distract from the work that needs to be done, while not actually requiring their input.

To this end, the new EA needs to be confident in acting unilaterally and independently. They need to know when to make decisions that their executive will be happy for them to make, without disturbing the executive. We will talk about this more in terms of priorities management and acting as a conduit of information flow and access, but the important concept here is that as a trusted partner an EA should be able to manage and handle, on their own, a lot of the day-to-day 'stuff' of any office.

Furthermore, by developing greater business acumen and business management skills, greater industry and corporate knowledge, and more in-depth strategic understanding of the executive's projects and priorities, a great EA will learn how to be proactive in anticipating the needs of the executive. An assistant at this level will be able to seek out information, communicate with a colleague or arrange a meeting before their executive has made a request for them to do so. Perhaps even before the executive realised this was what they needed!

Again, we will go into this in much more detail, but suffice to say for now that the key concept here is that a great EA will be so in tune with their executive that they rarely need to be asked for anything or to do anything. This EA knows what their executive is working on and what to get them before they need it. And they are confident enough in their understanding of the business and priorities, and in how their executive would respond or react to a given situation, to make a decision themselves (or redirect it, as we will discuss in Chapter 5) to avoid interrupting the executive.

The brand of the executive office

The concept of 'personal brand' and how essential it is to have one in business these days has been the subject of countless articles and workshops in recent years. Indeed most experts now argue that whether you have been cultivating one or not, your 'brand' exists anyway. It is essentially how people see you or perceive you in a business context, who they think you are and what they think you stand for. There is obviously much more to it than that, but that summary is sufficient for our purposes.

What I want to introduce here is the notion of a 'brand' of the executive office.

Once a strong working partnership starts to evolve between an executive and their EA, and the EA begins to act effectively as the manager of the executive's office, it is amazing how quickly the entity of the office – in essence the embodiment of the partnership of the EA and the executive – starts to take on its own persona.

People start to think of the partnership – the office – as the entity they need to deal with, rather than that being an individual. This is important in the context of trust in ensuring that the executive's direct reports, those in other divisions or areas, as well as other key stakeholders, start to realise that the EA is the most effective person for them to address in the first instance on almost every issue.

Clearly this has a lot to do with trust and how the EA builds and manages those relationships. Again, we will discuss this much more, but the concept I want to introduce here is that while an EA and their executive will maintain their own personal brands, and these won't be the same, those brands need to be congruent and aligned sufficiently that they are consistent with the 'combined' brand of their partnership. If not, it will be difficult for the brand of the office to gel.

In the next chapter we will discuss individuals' values from the perspective of the establishment of trust between an EA and an executive. These are vital when it comes to having an aligned brand. Our values are some of the most deep-seated determinants of behaviours and working styles or approaches and these will have a huge impact on how easy it is for an EA and an executive to develop a strong working partnership, and in turn a powerful brand for their office.

2

A true partnership based on trust

AT THE VERY CENTRE OF OUR EA-Executive Partnership Model is a foundation of trust – the basis of the EA-executive partnership. The quicker and more deeply trust can be engendered in a new relationship, the faster that relationship can evolve into a truly effective working partnership.

In the EA-executive partnership, trust is needed on a number of levels. Most EAs are privy to all manner of confidences and sensitive information, not to mention private communications and insights into the real nature of political alliances. There is the obvious need for an EA to be discreet and to maintain confidences. At a more subtle level, trust is the key ingredient that will ultimately allow an executive to comfortably let his or her EA work without supervision, work autonomously and make decisions unilaterally. When trust exists, the EA will have the confidence to work proactively, anticipate needs and make decisions to foreshadow requirements, to predict future courses of action and even to take on projects or direct activities without their executive needing to be constantly consulted.

Don't let trust just evolve

One of the great challenges of building trust and maintaining strong, long-term relationships in the workplace is that we tend to see those relationships as 'business' and therefore as something quite separate from our personal relationships. There are good reasons for this, of course. Workplace relationships exist primarily in order to get things done, whereas our personal relationships are more about providing company and support to one another.

Workplace relationships also tend to be more impermanent, of course. A consequence of this distinction is that we tend not to invest the same amount of time and emotional effort in building trust in our workplace relationships. Almost always, the deeper aspects of such relationships – including the level of trust needed between an EA and their executive – are allowed to simply evolve over time.

Whenever we have asked executives how long it generally takes for trust to evolve between themselves and a new EA – trust in the assistant's decision-making abilities, their insights and suggestions, and sufficient trust to allow them to work alongside the executive in a true partnership – the answer is generally somewhere between 12 and 24 months, with an average period of just under 18 months.

When you consider that many executives spend only around two-and-a-half years in any given role, as do many EAs, we have a situation in which very few EA-executive relationships ever reach the point of operating as a truly effective partnership. That's not to say that executives and their assistants are not working reasonably efficiently together, but rather that few of them reach an optimum level in their working relationship. This equates to a significant executive workload that might have been delegated or otherwise avoided had a level of complete trust been reached more quickly.

When we then ask why trust can't be reached in a shorter time, the typical answer is that trust takes time to evolve, and it needs to be allowed to evolve organically.

I believe this is highly inefficient. There is every reason for executives and their EAs to take steps, right from the outset, to proactively build trust in their relationship as quickly as they can. And our experience is that there are effective ways that this can be done.

A model for developing trust in an EA-executive partnership

Numerous models for building trust exist and they all share many common features. The most important elements are based around:

- shared intent and expectations
- values
- integrity
- competence and capabilities
- delivery and assessment.

These elements build on each other, as illustrated in Figure 3. With an understanding of them and how they combine to establish trust, it is possible to initiate a conscious program for fast-tracking the development of trust.

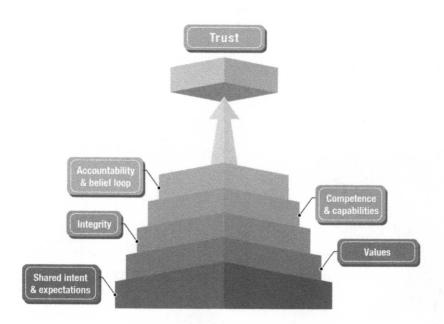

Figure 3: Development of trust

In our Network we train assistants in a process that is based largely on the 'shared intent and expectations' level, as getting this right is fundamental to further progress. Our approach involves a five-stage learning and feedback loop. Once that loop is working effectively, advancement can be made at the other levels.

Shared intent and expectations

Misalignment and miscommunication are two of the most significant factors that will constrain the development of trust in any relationship. If they are allowed to continue in a working relationship, the point of true partnership will never be reached.

It is for this reason that our approach places early emphasis on achieving alignment of purpose and expectations. In our training work we have executives and their assistants complete a pre-course survey designed to help identify any areas of existing misalignment in terms of intent, vision and purpose, and also any areas in which communication may be lacking.

Our five-stage loop process is designed to help build, and then constantly reinforce, agreements and commitments made in respect of intent, boundaries, beliefs and communication. This helps to build trust proactively rather than simply letting it evolve. The process is summarised in Figure 4. The remaining chapters in this book will provide the background you need to 'fill out' each of these areas, but for now I will provide an overview.

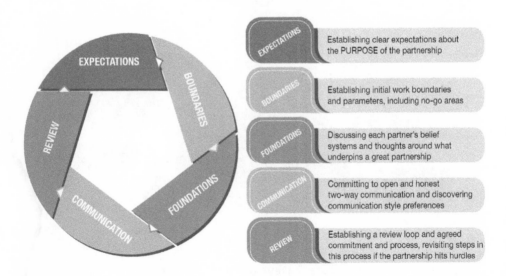

Figure 4: Building and maintaining shared intent and expectations

Step 1 – Establishing clear expectations about the purpose of the partnership and what it is expected to achieve and deliver

It may seem to be stating the obvious to say that developing shared intent and expectations requires an executive and his or her EA to sit down and have a conversation. Sadly, for something so 'obvious' this is rarely done, or at least not in sufficient depth. With the constant pressure for any new or newly promoted employee to 'hit the ground running', establishing clear expectations is all too often left to chance. This in turn leads to unintentional disappointments as both parties stumble along in the early months, feeling their way while they try to establish a jointly understood purpose, objectives and intent for the role over time.

It is absolutely imperative for EAs and executives to devote early – and sufficient – time to having a very clear conversation about the nature of the EA role, what it is designed to achieve and exactly where both parties see it adding value to the executive. Similar check-in conversations with the same purpose need to occur on a regular, ongoing basis.

Aligned to these discussions is the issue of the position description. The position description should be a document designed to help clarify the purpose and intent of the EA role. As already mentioned, it should not simply be a list of basic duties, as is so often the case (while often also being outdated). Starting with an inadequate position description sets back the aim of establishing shared expectations from the outset. In contrast, a good position description provides a framework for the EA's role that becomes a truly useful document in the clarification and re-clarification of shared intent and expectations.

Step 2 – Establishing initial work boundaries and parameters, including no-go areas

Mutually understood boundaries and no-go areas – while essential to shared intent and expectations – can be challenging things to establish, particularly in the early days of a new EA-executive partnership. What actions can the EA take without consulting their executive? Who should have direct and immediate access to the executive and who shouldn't? What limits are there on what the EA can do with their executive's diary?

Of course there are no cut-and-dried answers to questions like these. Even where the overall framework of intent, purpose and objectives are the same, boundaries will vary in each case due to the unique responsibilities of a particular executive, the industry they are in and, of course, the working style and preferences of the executive themselves.

Where boundaries are drawn they will also depend on the strengths, abilities and previous experiences of the executive and of the assistant. Very few people are so well rounded and evolved that they are strong in every aspect of their character, skills and knowledge within a business context; EAs and executives need to consider each other's relative strengths when deciding what's in and what's out. The executive's previous experiences with EAs may influence which areas of their work they are willing to delegate. So might their individual predilections and personal biases in terms of what the EA role should be.

The important thing here is not necessarily that each party understands why boundaries and no-go areas are drawn where they are, but that they are drawn and that they are understood. Over time, as trust deepens and the partnership evolves, these boundaries will typically change – which is why they need to be revisited at regular intervals. But they must be established at the outset.

Step 3 – Foundations: discussing each partner's belief systems and thoughts around what underpins a great partnership

The notion of foundations is essentially about understanding what value an executive and their assistant each ascribe to different aspects of their shared vision and objectives, and how they will manage any differences. For instance, if an EA believes that accuracy and punctuality are the most important aspects of their mutual agreement, but the executive places higher value on the relationship, how might that affect the way the two of them work together? 'I'm always late, but we get on well so it's great', thinks the executive, while his assistant is thinking, 'It drives me nuts that she's never on time'.

These differences are not critical in and of themselves. Every aspect of the EA's role and of the EA-executive relationship is important. What is important is that the relative priorities of each partner are mutually understood and that both parties are willing to be accommodating of the other's preferences in working together.

These underpinning foundations of the EA-executive partnership are very closely aligned to the concept of values that we will discuss shortly. At this point we are focussing simply on the need to have a conversation around the relative importance of different aspects of the model to each party, as this will directly impact the effectiveness of working together in a partnership.

Step 4 – Committing to open and honest two-way communication and discovering communication style preferences

There will be no trust without communication. That is as true in working EA-executive relationships as it is in personal relationships, commercial relationships and even diplomatic relationships. Establishing and maintaining clear communication is the single biggest prerequisite for pre-empting and resolving differences. There are few disagreements that can't be sorted out if people communicate well together.

For the purposes of our approach, we see communication in terms of both capability and intent.

From a capability standpoint, studying and discussing each other's natural and preferred communication styles is important to help ensure that both EA and executive are approaching communication in ways that are mutually satisfactory, comfortable and effective. The topic of effective communication techniques is vast. There is an endless array of books, resources and tools available to provide guidance on the topic and delving into it in any detail is well beyond the scope of this book (though we do cover the subject extensively in our training programs). Suffice to say that if communication techniques are getting in the way of an EA-executive relationship there is plenty of help available.

However, it's one thing to be *able* to communicate – to have the skills to do so. It is quite another to have a *commitment* to doing so. And commitment, or intent, is at least as important, if not more so, as capability here. This is the starting point for putting into place an effective routine for dealing with issues and problems as part of a continual feedback loop.

When it comes to a partnership based on trust, it is absolutely vital that both parties commit to being open and honest in their communications with each other at all times. Totally open and honest, and with full transparency. It is equally important that this commitment is made in person to each other. There is a psychological reassurance that comes from sharing such an intent with someone, based on a shared and aligned vision. Inherently most of us understand this. We've all had situations in our lives in which there has been a temptation not to be open with someone, and most of us have felt the pangs of early mistrust that falling into that temptation can engender. A failure of trust is never far away in a relationship when one party perceives that the other is not being as open and honest as they might be, leading to a rapidly growing cycle of speculation, worry, anxiety and doubt.

It is important to have an early and frank conversation about intent and open communication that incorporates each other's preferred communication styles and methods. Share a commitment to being open, honest and upfront, to speaking up when an issue or 'blockage' arises. Then, importantly, commit to remaining that way.

Step 5 – Establishing a review loop and a policy for revisiting steps in the trust model process, particularly if the partnership hits hurdles

The first four steps of the cycle that have been described so far are all about establishing frameworks, boundaries and intent for the EA-executive partnership, with the purpose of proactively building trust in a timely manner with minimal misalignments or miscommunication.

The final step of the cycle is to commit to constantly reviewing these steps as the partnership evolves and as changes inevitably take place in the wider organisation. All four areas – expectations, boundaries and no-go areas, foundational beliefs about the purpose of the EA role, and communication effectiveness – need to be reviewed on a regular basis.

The review process is made much easier if there is a genuine commitment to open and honest two-way communication. Such a commitment sets the perfect tone for being able to review and evaluate change in a way that reinforces trust and the mutual desire for that trust to be maintained.

Steps 1 to 3 can be reviewed and discussed at any time, and should be ... frequently. Indeed, we believe that there should be formal and informal discussions on a regular basis until the partnership is well established and trust is well cemented in the way that both partners work together. When supported by a clear framework for what the EA role can be and achieve, like the one we have developed, these conversations become so much easier, much less nebulous or vague, and much clearer and more aligned.

Values

The second stage in the development of the trust model (Figure 3) is the sharing of values. Values are, simply put, what we hold as important in our lives, in the sense that they help to define who we are. They can be good or bad, depending on how you perceive them and, indeed, our perception of the relative 'goodness' or 'badness' of the values of others is determined by our own.

We are driven by our values in the sense that we do what we value, so they help shape what we prioritise in our lives.

From the point of view of building trust in an EA-executive partnership, understanding each other's values is an important component of understanding what drives, motivates and defines ourselves and the person we are working with.

There are hundreds of different values people can have, from courtesy to tolerance, compassion to vitality.

Some hold punctuality as an absolutely essential value while others give it less importance. Sometimes there is a cultural effect on values. In some cultures lateness is regarded as disrespectful, implying that you believe your time is more important than that of the person who is left waiting for you. Yet some people have a totally different perception of time and its importance and therefore find it really hard to place the same value on punctuality.

Another example might be someone who values accuracy over expediency, which may be completely opposite to the values of the person they are working with.

Given that values help define us and help define the priority we attach to certain behaviours or tasks, it stands to reason that when working alongside another person in a close partnership you need to understand what that person values and, importantly, try to avoid judging how those values affect their actions and decisions.

In relation to how this affects the establishment of trust, when both EA and executive are open to the idea of value differences and work to understand the values of each other, a strong bond can be established that demonstrates empathy, caring, loyalty and, of course, unity.

Integrity

From the perspective of building trust in a partnership, having integrity or being principled is all about the actions you take and the way you go about your work.

The Latin word 'integritas' means wholeness, coherence, rightness or purity. Integrity has been defined as consistency between word and deed – 'the perceived degree of congruence between the values expressed by words and those expressed through action'[1] – while the concept of having principles goes perhaps a bit further, in common usage often connecting to the morals underneath the action.

But perhaps this is all just semantics. The important thing here is to understand that the building of deep trust goes further than having shared, or at least mutually understood, values. Here we are talking about the manner in which you act and how people perceive that as being consistent with what you say and the moral standards to which you hold others. Reliability, honesty, fairness, consistency and loyalty would make it on to most people's list of positive values. But to be seen as being principled, or as having integrity, depends on whether you display these values in your actions as perceived by others.

---

1 Simons, Tony L. 1999 'Behavioral integrity as a critical ingredient for transformational leadership.' Journal of Organizational Change Management, 12: 89–104.

Bringing this back to the partnership between an EA and their executive and the building of trust, it's all about understanding each other's stated values at the outset, as we've discussed. Then, at the next level and over time, how well does each party perceive the other's level of adherence to those values through their actions – their integrity?

We are now at a point that is beyond discussion – it's time to live those values, and that really comes down to each person as an individual.

Competence and capabilities

The next stage in building trust relates to competence and capabilities.

For trust to exist in the partnership between an executive and their assistant, the partners need to believe that each has the ability to deliver on the expectations that were established for the partnership. Delivery is the final stage of the puzzle, but you can't deliver without the requisite knowledge, skills and experience.

In our EA-Executive Partnership Model, competence and capabilities are represented by the second ring around the inner core of the foundation of trust and of the brand of the executive office.

We will elaborate on these competencies and capabilities as they apply to the new EA, but they loosely cover the following areas:

- technical knowledge and skills

- extensive industry knowledge

- sound business acumen and business management understanding

- broad knowledge across the whole organisation and all facets and disciplines of work

- exceptional communications skills

- strong persuasiveness and/or sales skills

- negotiation skills

- high levels of emotional intelligence.

You may notice that this list is somewhat different from what you have seen in the position descriptions of PAs and EAs in the past, and even in many EA job descriptions today. For instance, there is much less emphasis on routine administrative work.

In the next chapter we will describe the exact profile of skills, knowledge and traits we believe is required of the new EA. For now, it is important to note that trust is enhanced every time someone delivers on what they said they were going to do, and diminished every time they fail to meet expectations. The more an EA can build on their capabilities and demonstrate them, the more their executive will have faith in their ability and entrust them to do more. And the more the EA delivers, the more trust will be built, making this a very productive cycle that we call the 'accountability and belief loop'.

Accountability and belief loop

We created the accountability and belief loop (Figure 5) to help us to understand how competence and capability work to build trust. The purpose of the loop is to show how, over time, trust in an assistant grows as the assistant continues to deliver on expectations. It's a powerful cycle whereby belief is repeatedly reinforced, to the point where there is no doubt that the EA will deliver. Reaching this point is a major factor in the development of trust in an EA-executive partnership.

Our loop has five simple stages. We believe that if both executive and EA are aware of these steps and are able to communicate using the language of the steps, the cycle can be accelerated and trust built more quickly.

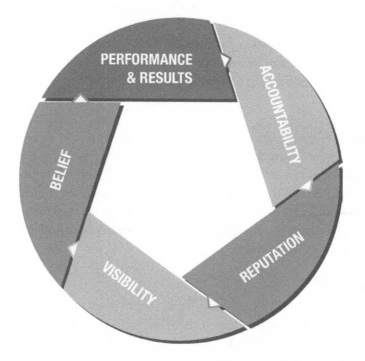

Figure 5: Accountability and belief loop

Performance and results

It should go without saying that achieving results is a fundamental part of the EA's role, if not *the* fundamental purpose of the role. This obviously goes well beyond the notion of building trust. The aim of building trust between EA and executive is ultimately because trust will allow the executive to achieve better performance – not the other way around.

However, when we talk about results, having a sound and mutually agreed way of measuring performance is essential. A situation in which the EA feels he or she has done a great job, but the executive sees the same performance as only mediocre, is hardly a great way to reinforce trust.

We will explore this topic in more detail in Chapter 11, but in terms of the accountability and belief loop, performance measurement needs to be aligned with the established aims of the EA's role and the extent to which the EA has helped the executive achieve their objectives.

Accountability

Once performance standards have been set, the assistant needs to be held accountable to those standards. There are few things more demoralising than being given a goal, only to have the goal posts move or, worse, be forgotten a few days later. Obviously accountability requires executive follow-up, with performance regularly reviewed, shortfalls against targets discussed and great or over-performance noted and rewarded. This is a good test of the robustness of the shared intent and expectations, values and communication that have been established between executive and assistant.

Reputation

As delivery improves and accountability is upheld, the EA will start to gain a reputation in their executive's mind for being consistently able to achieve on expectations. Conversely, the EA will gain greater confidence that they are 'doing the right thing'. As this occurs we tend to also see the EA's reputation grow in the eyes of others in the executive team and related stakeholders – an important step in the EA being able to act more unilaterally and proactively.

Visibility

Reputation builds visibility, and visibility reinforced by reputation equates to stature and position in the minds of others. This natural extension of reputation is about how the EA can extend their reach to more people in the sphere of the executive and ultimately to the wider organisation. This in turn provides a catalyst to the EA taking on a more significant leadership and management role in their own right and so becoming far more effective in their ability to assist the executive in achieving their goals and objectives.

Belief

Belief in someone is a very powerful emotion and absolutely the cornerstone of the final stage of trust-building between an executive and their assistant. When the point of 'belief' is reached, the partnership is typically working so well that the executive just knows they can rely totally on their EA to do or achieve anything asked of them and to manage any exigency or unexpected situation with a minimum of fuss or interruption of the executive, while obviously keeping the executive 'in the loop' to avoid unwanted surprises.

When all the other aspects of what we have outlined in this trust process have been put in place, establishing and then continually reinforcing that feeling of belief, that feeling of being able to rely and depend upon their assistant, is what ultimately leads to a truly strong and even essential partnership in the eyes of the executive.

Loyalty

Whenever I discuss issues of trust with senior executives and EAs, the issue of loyalty is always raised as well. Loyalty and trust go hand in hand. There cannot be ongoing trust without loyalty. In so many of the day-to-day activities of an EA, executives tacitly – and with complete justification – expect loyalty, whether that be the EA having their back and looking out for them, the way the EA deals with office politics, the way they manage any dealings with confidential business information and, of course, the way they deal with any private personal information about the executive, their family or other matters.

An EA working in partnership with an executive simply must be loyal, to the extent that the loyalty is both legal and morally justifiable.

Some would argue that any member of staff, not just EAs, in any organisation should be loyal first and foremost to that organisation and its best interests. While this premise does hold true most of the time, I do believe there are times when an executive would not be surprised by an individual who looked after their own interests first, especially where broader office politics come into play. Should someone be caught between the competing interests of different executives, for instance, they may find it difficult to work out where their loyalties should rest in the best interests of the organisation.

But again, this situation should be rare in the case of an EA whose loyalty lies with his or her own executive.

The only situations in which an EA would be justified in questioning their loyalty to their executive would be those in which the executive is doing something that is clearly immoral, unethical or, in extreme cases, illegal. Such a circumstance would clearly break down the framework of trust in the first instance. In those cases where the EA didn't believe they could address the issue directly with their executive, it would also leave them needing to consider very carefully how they should act and who they should consult for advice.

There are many texts that discuss loyalty in depth and the ways in which it can be both a positive and negative in certain business or organisational circumstances. As to providing clear guidance to EAs on how they should act in any hypothetical situation, that is beyond the scope of this book.

For now let's stick with the simple premise that for trust to exist and thrive between an EA and an executive, each party must demonstrate loyalty to the other.

3

The breadth of knowledge of a general manager, without the same depth?

EVER FOUND YOURSELF in the early days of a new job in a new organisation and needing the answer to a simple question or to know where to find something or how to get something done? Chances are you were directed to one of the executive assistants for the answer. Or perhaps you just went straight to them, knowing they would likely have the answer.

EAs are important repositories of knowledge in most organisations. No matter where they sit in the organisation, they know what happens where, who does what, where things are stored or filed and who can make things happen quickly and efficiently. The nature of the EA role is that it has connections at all levels in an organisation, both vertically and horizontally. This has been the case for decades, since EAs and PAs were 'secretaries' and 'typists'. Having *breadth* of knowledge – that is, knowing a bit about just about everything – is a facet of the EA role that hasn't changed, though we believe it is evolving.

The executive, by contrast, traditionally has *depth* of knowledge. They know a lot more about a lot fewer things than their EA. So the executive has a deep understanding of the reasons why a certain strategy is being followed, and of the ramifications if things change or that strategy doesn't work. The executive probably doesn't know who to call about the photocopier blowing up – they rely on their EA's breadth of knowledge for that.

As I've already discussed, and will be expanding on much more, the new EA is also the manager of the executive office. They work more autonomously and proactively than in the past, directing and managing rather than passively being assigned tasks or acting reactively. They are a facilitator of outcomes, a manager of priorities, a manager of their executive's energy flow, focus and mindset, a conduit of information and access, and a corporate thermometer.

To achieve all this the new EA requires the same breadth of knowledge they've always had, but a different, 'deeper' level of knowledge, information and skills in some important areas than has traditionally been the case. They need to understand not just what is happening at any time, but *why* different matters have different levels of importance and priority, what impacts on those priorities and what makes changes inevitable. They need to be able to analyse any knowledge, information and data they receive and assess how it will affect their executive's goals and priorities and those of the organisation. Ideally they'll be able to do this without having to interrupt their executive in the process.

At any time an EA should know what is keeping their executive awake at night and why, and have insight into how solutions for those problems can be formulated, by whom, and how they can assist.

This combination of breadth and depth of knowledge, skills and insight comes with experience, but also by having a sufficient level of general business knowledge and acumen along with an understanding of their organisation, where it sits in terms of current competitive pressures and market forces, and even the legislative and legal frameworks the organisation operates within or under.

There really isn't a limit to the level of knowledge, skills, acumen and insight an EA should develop. The more they know and understand, the better placed they will be to support their executive and the executive's team in achieving all their goals and objectives. Keep in mind that the new EA's key purpose is always to free up the executive from having to get involved too heavily in the minutiae, or sometimes even in more complex issues, unless they have to, thus allowing the executive to operate at their optimum level.

In this chapter I am going to focus on the second ring of the EA-Executive Partnership Model – on the skills, both technical and social, an EA should look to develop; what levels of corporate and industry knowledge they need; what general business acumen and management understanding and skills they should have; and what specific knowledge they need of the organisation or divisional area of which their executive is in charge.

In terms of business acumen and knowledge I will share the recipe for new EA success. I will highlight the many different areas they should aim to grasp so they can create their own strategic development plan to help them get there. I will also look at the social and interpersonal skills EAs need; these often offer the greatest potential to positively assist their executive. Finally, I will cover the basics: all those areas an EA needs to master and then build on to become even more indispensable, working truly alongside their executive.

All these elements will be expanded on in more detail in later chapters as I demonstrate how they can be put into action to achieve the different elements of our model of the new executive assistant's role.

Interpersonal skills, social skills and emotional intelligence

Whenever our organisation conducts a survey with executive assistants, the so-called 'soft skills' are rated as the most important: the ability to interact well with others, build relationships, communicate well, demonstrate sound emotional intelligence, read moods and deal with conflict. These are the things that EAs see as high priorities. Not surprisingly, emotional intelligence is rated highest among these. Very surprisingly, the vast majority of EAs claim to have never had any formal training in emotional intelligence or any of the other 'soft skills'. It's simply assumed that they will have them.

There are so many psychometric-type assessment tools that can be used to help EAs gain basic knowledge in all these areas, but that's never really going to be enough. EAs really need quite advanced interpersonal and social skills along with social awareness. That said, it's beyond the scope of this book to provide detailed guidance and instruction in these areas – that's the domain of countless other books, workshops and training courses. What I can do is expand on those areas that the new EA really should have competence in.

Personal skills and traits

Hopefully it's becoming clear that the successful new executive assistant is someone who possesses a wide range of skills, many of which are personal skills or traits. No single list can completely do justice to the skills required of the job, and of course there are many personal traits that are difficult to learn if they don't come naturally to you. Nevertheless, below are some of the more important skills and traits I believe EAs should possess and, where possible, continue to strengthen. These are presented in alphabetical order rather than order of importance.

Assertiveness – Assertiveness is going to be essential from time to time when the EA is working alongside an executive, managing their office and taking a leadership role in helping them to achieve the best possible outcomes, particularly when at times the EA is going to have to operate unilaterally.

Consistency – When an EA is consistent in terms of their approach and delivery, they will find that earning trust and belief from those they work with, internally and externally, comes much more easily. Having a consistent manner and acting with consistent professionalism and attitude will take this further, smoothing the way to facilitate the outcomes the executive is aiming for while also strengthening the brand of the executive office.

Consultation – Any leader knows that achieving the best outcomes requires a good level of consultation and a willingness to work with others. And as I've made clear, leadership is an essential component of the new EA's role. In managing the office of the executive, the EA needs to be able to listen to others and consult on their intentions, goals and desired outcomes.

Cooperation – Being a team player is as much about cooperation as it is about consulting and listening. It follows that, in acting as a proxy for the executive at times, the EA will need to be able to cooperate with others on their executive's team.

Diplomacy – Diplomacy is an important aspect in any role, particularly towards the 'top' of an organisation. For the EA, sitting as they do 'between' the executive and the rest of the organisation, and often as the conduit between the two, the ability to be diplomatic is arguably more important still. EAs frequently deal with sensitive information and personal matters so they need to be extremely careful in how they handle these situations. The EA also needs to be diplomatic when passing on directives or instructions on behalf of their executive or asking for information on their behalf, and of course when seeking to deflect those looking to access the executive or pass on information to them.

Discernment – Using sound judgment to distinguish between what is important or vital and what is less so is as much about understanding the relative importance of competing priorities as it is about the EA using their personal judgment, based on experience and understanding of the emotions and personalities involved. From the EA perspective, being discerning involves thinking beyond the technical and the practical to the impact of situations and decisions on every level and making sound judgments based on this.

Discretion – From dealing with confidential business information to highly sensitive personal information, the EA will come across an inordinate amount of information and data that has to be handled with complete discretion. There is no room for ambiguity here: a single act of indiscretion can destroy years of hard-earned trust.

Empathy – Sitting alongside emotional intelligence, having the ability to put yourself in the shoes of others is a vital part of the EA toolkit when it comes to building strong relationships with the executive, his or her key team members and other staff, as well as with other internal and external stakeholders. Empathy is even more important on those occasions when the EA needs to take on a leadership or management role. Empathy will improve over time as the EA better understands the pressures that individuals feel in their specific roles, but this is also one area that every EA should work on proactively if they feel they are falling short in it.

Inquisitiveness – This is perhaps a less obvious trait than some of the others in this list. The point here is about being proactive rather than reactive, leading and managing rather than being directed. Achieving this requires an open mind and an inquisitive nature that actively wants to understand the 'why' behind any situation. What are the reasons and motivations driving any particular decision? The more the EA knows this, the better placed they will be to predict how their executive will respond to a given situation, and that will help the EA to be more proactive.

Motivation – This may not seem an obvious part of the EA role. However, more and more organisations are seeing the benefits, particularly during times of change, of using EA connections throughout the organisation to motivate others and keep their morale high. Beyond that, the EA often needs to be able to motivate in terms of pushing for people to hit project targets or even targets for the submission of reports or data.

Patience – A consequence of having the reputation of being the go-to person, or being seen as a doer, is that many EAs always want to act now – to forge ahead and get things done. However, the role of the new EA as manager of the executive office requires that they learn to play a longer game and have patience, because sometimes things need to happen at different times for a reason – a more strategically focussed reason.

Personableness – Antonyms to personable include disagreeable, sullen and surly. While these terms may have been used to describe many of the 'gatekeeper' EAs of yesteryear ('pitbulls with lipstick' I have heard them referred to as), this approach won't work for the new EA, who is aiming to be a facilitator of outcomes working alongside their executive as opposed to in front of them. I will talk in Chapter 6 about those times when the EA needs to be a protector of their executive, including sometimes being a necessary road block, but even when these are the case, maintaining a personable approach is important for the maintenance of relationships.

Persuasiveness – Playing a more active role in helping to deliver on outcomes means that the EA should take their part in selling ideas, concepts, plans and strategies. To do this they need to have strong persuasion skills to encourage others to buy in to what they are 'selling'.

Reliability – Being dependable, someone the executive and their team can rely on, is aligned with being consistent, because you have to do this not just once, but all the time. It is also aligned with having people develop belief in what they expect the EA to do, which, as I discussed in the previous chapter, is essential for building and maintaining trust.

Resilience – In today's constantly evolving business and regulatory environments, change is more common than ever before. When working alongside senior executives, this change and its impact can be more acutely felt. Resilience is now one of the buzz phrases in organisational professional development circles but as an EA dealing with change, and the pressures and emotional impacts of change on themselves and others in their team, resilience is essential if they are to thrive and not burn out.

Resourcefulness – The new executive assistant is more involved in actively helping their executive and their team achieve outcomes in all manner of project areas, along with other deliverables in the organisation. As a result, the EA has to be even more resourceful than they may have been in the past, knowing where to find the answers and solutions needed to get things done. This resourcefulness is heavily aligned to the knowledge areas I will expand on later in this chapter in terms of the EA's 'recipe for success'.

Sociability – Your willingness to interact with others is a direct measure of how sociable you are. The very essence of being a facilitator of results is determined by this. It's all about the EA's ability to network and build strong relationships throughout the organisation and with stakeholders both internally and externally. I'll expand on this in later chapters. If this 'sociable' side doesn't come naturally to an EA, it's something they're going to need to work on.

Tenacity – The ability to keep going and not to give up, often in the face of pressure or in difficult situations, is essential for everyone at a senior level in an organisation – which effectively means the EAs as well. Working in partnership with an executive means an EA needs to be as tenacious as the executive, prepared to take knocks, get back up and soldier on.

Trustworthiness – Where discretion is the ability to keep sensitive personal or business information confidential, and reliability is about others knowing that you'll do what you say you will do, being trustworthy goes a little further and literally means being worthy of trust. It is a matter of perception, and we saw in Chapter 2 the lengths one needs to go to to actually build trust. Needless to say, it is essential for the EA that others see them as being worthy of their trust. This takes time and effort, as we've discussed.

Emotional intelligence

In 1998, Daniel Goleman, who popularised the concept of emotional intelligence, wrote an article that quickly became a *Harvard Business Review* classic. In the article, entitled 'What makes a leader?', he discusses the importance of emotional intelligence as it relates to success in leadership in business.

> The most effective leaders are all alike in one crucial way: they all have a high degree of what has come to be known as emotional intelligence. It's not that IQ and technical skills are irrelevant. They do matter, but ... they are the entry-level requirements for executive positions. My research, along with other recent studies, clearly shows that emotional intelligence is the sine qua non of leadership. Without it, a person can have the best training in the world, an incisive, analytical mind, and an endless supply of smart ideas, but he still won't make a great leader.

Goleman then lists five components of emotional intelligence that allow individuals to recognise, connect with and learn from their own and other people's mental states: self-awareness, self-regulation, motivation, empathy and social skill.

While Goleman was in this instance writing about leadership, the points he makes are equally valid to EAs as we've been describing the modern role, with the need to be able to work effectively with large numbers of people inside and outside their organisation while also managing the office of their executive.

Simply put, emotional intelligence is the ability to recognise, understand and manage our own emotions while also being capable of recognising, understanding and influencing the emotions of others. In practice, this means being aware that emotions can shape our behaviour and affect people, both positively and negatively. It also means understanding that we need to learn how to manage the emotions of ourselves and others, especially when we are under pressure.

In terms of personal development, it's important to know that emotional intelligence (as opposed to the 'intelligence' measured in IQ tests) can be improved over time. It's not something we are born with and 'stuck' with thereafter. From this perspective we strongly encourage the EAs we work with to undertake some form of training or education that can help them learn how to keep improving their emotional intelligence.

Communication skills

In Chapter 2 I spent some time discussing the importance of communication in the building and maintenance of trust between an executive and their EA. However, it should be obvious that the need for communication skills goes far beyond trust. In many ways the role of the new EA is all about communication skills.

We all know of relationships that have floundered because of 'broken' communication, whether we were in those relationships ourselves or have seen this happen to others. Even if there are underlying issues other than poor communication, you can almost guarantee that those other issues can't be resolved without effective communication.

Given the complexity of the modern executive's role, the complexity of the issues that come to the executive office and, in turn, the complexity of the new EA role, communication between an executive and their assistant – both written and verbal – needs to be very frequent and very effective so that important issues are not missed or overlooked and misunderstandings don't develop. For this to happen both executive and EA need to have highly developed communication skills.

Leadership skills

Contrary to what many believe in business, commerce and government, leadership skills are not just the preserve of those in so-called leadership positions. At times everyone needs to take a leadership approach in their dealings with their colleagues, clients or key stakeholders.

I should make a distinction here between leadership and management. These are very different and shouldn't be confused, particularly in terms of the running of the executive office. 'Management' concerns the practicalities of organising resources to achieve objectives, whereas 'leadership' is about affecting the hearts and minds of the people we interact with.

Again, it is outside the scope of this book to fully delve into the topic of leadership – as you are probably well aware, there are scores of books dedicated entirely to this topic, from many different perspectives. What I do want to do is demonstrate why EAs need to develop leadership skills in addition to management skills if they are to proactively manage the office of their executive. It's all about getting others to 'buy in' to the plans, actions, strategies and vision that you will find yourself promoting on behalf of your executive. As an EA, there will be times when you can rely on the delegated authority of your executive to simply expect that someone will follow your directives. However, at other times you will need to draw on your own leadership skills to encourage people to 'follow you on the ride'.

I will talk in Chapter 10 about power and authority and the extent to which the EA needs a degree of delegated authority from the executive, but the new EA also needs to earn their own level of authority. This is where leadership comes in.

Conflict resolution skills

It hardly needs to be said that conflict is inevitable in any organisation. I challenge you to find any business, big or small, in which 'sweetness and light' prevail. People will always differ in their personal versions of the company's vision, and in their opinions about how that should be pursued. People will always compete over access to finite resources or to the limited time of senior executives. And of course there will always be clashes of personality, of working style, of communication style, and so on.

In one sense the new executive assistant needs to sit above all of this, maintaining focus on the goals of their executive and the organisation. However, as we've already discussed, a significant requirement for doing that is the building and maintenance of good working relationships with many people throughout the organisation. Being drawn into some level of conflict from time to time is inescapable for the EA, particularly on those occasions when they need to take a stand on some issue or other. There will be times when they find themselves in the firing line, even if they are just the messenger.

In many ways, being able to handle and manage conflict requires a combination of the communication and leadership skills I have already mentioned, though there are unique aspects to conflict resolution as well. Continuing to improve your conflict resolution skills will certainly help you become a more effective EA.

Management skills

Being an effective manager is probably the 'original' skill of the personal assistant, though I would argue that the level of management skill required of the new executive assistant is much higher than it used to be. This is simply a reflection of the greater complexity of the modern executive's role. The EA needs to be highly adept at the planning and direction of events and meetings, and at performing these tasks in a strategic manner that makes the best use of the available resources – including, especially, their executive's time. The best EAs will be recognised throughout the organisation for their management skills in this area.

As with leadership, there are scores of texts devoted to the pursuit of management, so I won't elaborate on it extensively here. Suffice to reinforce the point that EAs need to continually improve their management skills, even when they feel they are well established. And I will, in following chapters, refer to the art of management frequently as we dig into the specific management functions of the new EA from a practical standpoint.

An EA's recipe for success

Earlier I mentioned the distinction between 'breadth' and 'depth' of knowledge, the point being that the new EA needs the breadth of knowledge of a traditional PA while also having deeper knowledge in critical areas of the business than in the past. The more an EA understands of what an executive does, and importantly why they do what they do and why they make the decisions they make, the more the EA will be able to work proactively to offer support and help to manage competing priorities.

The scope of the different areas an EA should seek to gain knowledge and skills within is vast, and it will also be highly specific to each role and each organisation. As such, I can't get into specifics in this book. However, I can highlight the main areas in which most EAs will need a basic level of knowledge that can be further developed over time. My experience would suggest that an EA who has some grasp of all the areas described below will have a sound basis for success in their role, and that if this knowledge continues to evolve then ongoing success is more likely to follow.

It's a long list, and it won't happen overnight, but when taken as a whole it does provide a recipe for EA success.

1. Strategic planning

2. Project management

3. Internal stakeholder management

4. External stakeholder management

5. Team and direct reports management

6. Short-, medium- and long-term strategic objectives

7. The link between mission statement, strategic objectives and tactics in the executive's role

8. Major financial reports

9. Key factors influencing revenue, profitability and return on investment

10. Public, media and social media perceptions

11. Marketing initiatives and sales strategies

12. Corporate governance

13. Risk and compliance

14. Competitive analysis

15. Staff and resourcing issues

16. Overheads and business costs

17. Business administration

18. Executive's reputation and brand.

Mastering the basics

In Chapter 1 I lamented the quality of the position description many EAs have for their roles, most being little more than a list of tasks and responsibilities that most business support staff have had responsibility for over the past couple of decades, or more. It should be clear by now that I see the role of the new EA as much more than these basic tasks. However, that doesn't mean that they don't remain important.

While new technologies and software constantly change the way EAs operate, and the ways in which they fulfil the basic objectives – whether they are managing and organising diaries or arranging travel, for example – the necessity of these tasks hasn't changed. If nothing else, it doesn't make financial sense for a senior executive to focus time and energy on basic tasks that an assistant can do for them.

So the basics of the assistant's job are still the basics, and clearly *every* assistant must master the basics as a minimum, before they can contemplate adding many of the more strategically focussed, intangible aspects of the role that are the focus of this book.

That said, there are some organisations in which EAs are taking on more of a strategically focussed role in managing their executive office, effectively acting in more of a management capacity in their own right. In these cases the EA will typically have one or more junior assistants reporting to them and taking on responsibility for these basic tasks.

The following list does not by any means include all functions and tasks of an EA, but it does cover the main broad areas. What I hope to highlight here is how these can be understood in a more strategic sense and extended to more effectively enable the executive to be as dissociated as possible from these.

Computer literacy

In the category of computer literacy I include software knowledge and the use of both general and proprietary computer programs and systems.

It hardly needs to be said that survival in any modern organisation requires a reasonable level of knowledge and understanding of technology and well-developed computer skills – particularly for those involved in management and administration, and even more so for EAs. The focus has shifted in recent years. Today, EAs need to focus on how they can embrace constantly evolving technological solutions and make best use of them in their own work practices and those of their executive. Many EAs will also find themselves in the role of educator here, teaching the executive how to use the latest iPhone update, for instance.

Diary management

Once upon a time a meeting was something an executive would have in a room with other people. The only viable alternative was a telephone meeting, and even that used to require an office. Most meetings were organised at least a day or two ahead of time, and often longer.

Today, a 'meeting' can be held literally anywhere, the relative locations of the participants is irrelevant except for the necessary consideration of time zones. One person might be in front of a computer, another in a video conferencing facility and another joining in via the video capabilities of their mobile phone. Even being in the air is, increasingly, no excuse.

More meeting possibilities inevitably seem to lead to more meetings, which makes the EA's role in diary management all the more important. It's a task made more complex because of the variety of possible meeting formats – a factor not only in the management of the executive's diary but also that of the assistant. And on top of that today's shared digital diary means that the EA does not have the complete control that they may once have had.

The other change, as I've touched on, relates to the EA's role in managing their executive's time, not just their diary. Where once a secretary simply scheduled meetings at the request of an executive, the new EA will often be scheduling time on behalf of their executive without direct consultation with him or her. This won't just be for meetings. Today's EA will often need to be proactive in scheduling time for their executive to complete specific tasks, to have planning and thinking time and to have research and analysis time, depending on the needs of their role. Some of this comes down to 'protecting' the executive by helping to maintain their physiological health and meet their psychological needs, which I'll come back to.

Travel management

From simple local trips to interstate and international travel, organising and managing executive travel is a base component for almost every EA, a responsibility that clearly sits alongside diary management.

Time management

Closely aligned with diary management is time management. Where diary management is about the practicalities of scheduling, time management is about making effective use of time as a resource and, of course, minimising any wasted time. The executive needs to take some responsibility here, as effective time management is as much about management of self, or self-mastery, as anything else. It requires the ability to know yourself and how you work best, and to do what is necessary to organise your time around these factors. Both the executive and their assistant need to be competent managers of their time, and each needs to also understand the other's preferences in this area.

Managing communication flows

Like diary management, management of the flow of communication into and out of the executive office has become more complex, given the increased number of communication options. Communication flow and the EA's role in managing it can also be a source of contention when there are different interpretations of the importance of a particular message. We'll discuss this a lot in Chapter 5, but for now let's understand that at some level all EAs are involved in managing various aspects of communication.

An interesting aspect of communication management is the variety of potential levels of access an executive may or may not grant their assistant. There are executives who will not allow their EA access to their email inbox, for instance. This is increasingly rare, which is a good thing, given the shared executive-EA objective of managing executive priorities, focus and energy levels and minimising executive distraction. However, it is something that needs to be negotiated between the executive and their assistant.

Filing and knowledge management

As the go-to people for knowledge and information, EAs need to be good at filing information, knowledge reports and all other data that is important, or could be important, to the effective running of the business. This is important not only from the record-keeping perspective but simply as a practicality of their role. Again the main change here is the transition to digital files and the dream of the so-called 'paperless office'.

Thinking about how an EA might approach file and knowledge management from the more intangible aspects of the new EA role, we can look to the assistant's role in deciding the relative importance of information and making a call on what needs to remain accessible and what can be archived, rather than simply keeping all information in one large 'bucket', which makes finding anything much more difficult.

Data collection

Filing information and knowledge and ensuring it is readily accessible for those who need it is one skill. Knowing what data is required and where to find it is another. The EA will become more effective at this as they broaden and deepen their knowledge of the activities of the organisation and what the executive and their team are focussed on. The EA should strive to remain one step ahead, identifying potentially important data and storing it accessibly.

Taking notes and minutes

Until such time as electronic recording and transcription technology becomes completely reliable – and perhaps even beyond that for meetings where electronic recordings would never be acceptable – EAs will likely have a role in taking meeting notes and minutes. Of course, in an ideal world the new EA should be contributing to meetings as well as just recording their most salient points and issues, but this will not always be the case. That said, when EAs are taking notes or minutes the extent to which they understand the proceedings will have a bearing on the effectiveness of the record they capture and their ability to follow up on commitments post-meeting.

Research and analysis

The role of the EA has always had a minor amount of research and analysis assigned to it, though it has traditionally been fairly basic, and then only at the specific request of the executive. In our model, we believe this is an area where the new EA can make an extensive contribution. When taking on projects or assignments, or even in just assessing submissions of information to the executive office, if an EA can take on the role of analysing data and ensuring it is accurate, and can then make assessments and recommendations based on that data, they will be adding substantial value to their executive. I will discuss this further in relation to the EA's role in managing information and communication flow, and their role in protecting the executive and managing their priorities.

4

Staying one step ahead

How the new EA can direct the activities and priorities of the executive office

LIFE IN THE EXECUTIVE OFFICE, as both executives and their assistants know only too well, is a constant battle between making plans on the one hand and shuffling those plans around when the unexpected inevitably strikes. It's like mapping out a road trip only to have to constantly reroute due to traffic jams and roadworks appearing without warning. And while the promise of technology was once that it would help to improve visibility and smooth the way, the reality is that technology has mainly just made things a whole lot faster, or at least that's how it feels.

This environment is a big reason why the new executive assistant needs to play the more proactive and managing role that I have mentioned a number of times so far. It's why today's EA needs to be proactive, not only in managing their executive's time and priorities, but also in managing their energy, focus and relationships against the never-ending onslaught that seeks to prevent anything ever actually being done.

The ultimate goal here is to remove the need for an executive to be immersed in every detail of what is happening around them so they can remain focussed on higher-level strategic and intellectually challenging issues. The executive may know there is noise out there, but they also know they can safely ignore that noise in the knowledge that their EA is keeping distractions at bay unless absolutely necessary.

Of course, doing this 'filtering' job successfully requires that the EA has a significant and clear understanding of the relative importance of the executive's competing priorities, challenges, threats and opportunities. The EA needs to be able to assess all information and data they receive and make a judgment call as to whether to alert their executive immediately, later at a more convenient time (i.e. without interrupting the executive's train of thought) or not at all. This is why they need the sorts of knowledge described in the last chapter. The better the EA understands where a piece of information or data sits in terms of priority in the mind of the executive, the more confidently the EA can act.

Obviously there are potential major incidents that will require urgent interruption. The challenge is in dealing with more subtle issues where, say, the EA becomes privy to something that is happening that others may not be aware of. These may include human capital or personnel situations, information coming to light in relation to a specific project, or even an upcoming event or trip. At times the need to reprioritise executive focus and activities may not be so obvious, and of course there will always be limits to how far anyone can read another person's mind! Nevertheless, the clearer the EA is in their understanding of their executive's objectives and goals, the better placed they'll be to make the right call.

And, once again, I can't overstate the importance of ongoing communication here. Being able to regularly discuss incoming information and data with their executive will help to continually improve the EA's understanding of their boss's thinking on various issues. So too will regular conversations in which the EA is able to question their executive to get their take on where priorities and focus should lie at that exact time. These conversations will also play a role in building the executive's trust in their EA's ability to make appropriate 'triage' decisions.

Being proactive in making priority and judgment calls as I've been describing requires that the EA develop a healthy regard for, and acceptance of the need for, risk taking. This applies as much to filtering information as it does to handling requests for meetings – particularly where the person making the request is a customer or someone internal but more senior to the EA. This, of course, comes in part from experience and knowledge – the same things that allow executives themselves to take risks. It also comes from knowing the degree to which the EA is trusted to make the right decision. And as with anything, the willingness to take risks will also depend on being clear about the consequences should a mistake be made, and of the possible alternative actions that could be taken to mitigate those consequences if necessary. The executive who is able to forgive mistakes when they are made despite the best intentions, and to see them as a learning opportunity, is more likely to have an EA who is willing to risk making a mistake. Risks can't always pay off or they wouldn't be risks. That's business.

Another point I need to make is that there is no 'one size fits all' here. The nimble EA-executive partnership in which an EA is able to make many day-to-day decisions on behalf of their executive won't suit every organisational culture. In some larger corporations and government departments, slow and steady is the preferred approach and any significant decision needs to be run past multiple chains of command, so to speak. An EA therefore needs to be fairly sure not only of how their executive would react in a given situation, but also how the organisation as a whole would act. This is another component of the trust-building process that I discussed in Chapter 2. And it's another reason why ongoing communication is so necessary.

In an ideal situation, an EA needs to know what it is that keeps their boss awake at night, metaphorically speaking. In the best situations there will be nothing literally keeping the executive awake, but most will have one or two issues at any time weighing on their minds more heavily than others. When the EA knows what these are, they will be in a better position to provide proactive assistance.

In this chapter we move into the outer circle of the EA-Executive Partnership Model, and in particular to the areas of strategic planning and project management.

Strategic objectives versus short-term objectives

Over the years we have often asked both EAs and executives whether or not the EA has any involvement in strategic planning meetings. In most cases we learn that EAs either have no involvement in these meetings or, if they do, it is only to organise the meeting and perhaps take minutes or notes.

This is yet another example of the prevailing but old-fashioned approach to the role of the EA. It should be clear by now that it is certainly not consistent with what I see as the role of the new EA: essentially to have the EA effectively managing the executive's energy, focus, mindset, priorities and relationships. And as I've just explained, that means the assistant needs to know what's going on ... and at more than a superficial level.

Once an EA has the basic knowledge, skills and business acumen required, their involvement at strategic planning meetings is all about adding context, or 'depth', to that knowledge. This is where the EA can start to understand the 'why' behind the decisions their executive and the executive team are making and why the organisation is being taken in the chosen direction. They will better understand the priorities driving short-term objectives as well as what the longer-term objectives are. And they will understand the 'how': the intended strategies for actually delivering against those plans.

When an EA has this context they are in a much better position to play their role in communication with the wider organisation. They will be better able to understand the potential impact of chosen strategies on different departments, divisions, teams and personnel – and the likely reactions to those impacts.

In our experience the best way for EAs to gain this context is for them to not only attend strategic planning meetings but to actively participate in them, asking questions and, where appropriate, even providing their own insights and thoughts as their knowledge, understanding and confidence grows. This is quite a step beyond simply taking notes, and it is an important step in the role of the new executive assistant.

Project planning

There have been various circumstances in which we have found EAs being involved with specific projects within organisations. This is not surprising, given discrete projects are increasingly used as a targeted and measurable way of contributing to larger organisational objectives.

The first time we came across an EA actively involved in scoping and conducting research for a specific project was in 2008. The company was a boutique funds management firm and the EA was heavily involved in the development of a major disaster recovery plan for the site. At the time we found the EA's level of involvement unusual. The typical EA role in a project plan was minute taking in meetings and not much more. However, in recent years we have come across other EAs who have been tasked with very similar projects. Other common projects for EAs to be heavily involved with, if not actually running themselves, are office relocations.

In many instances like this the EA was given more hands-on and strategic involvement in a project because they wanted to gain the experience and so volunteered for the task. But in other cases we know assistants who have been asked to participate because their executive wanted someone they could trust to be closely involved, with a good knowledge of what was happening and the ability to keep the executive abreast of progress.

The new EA needs to be in touch with current projects for all the reasons I've discussed so far, including transparency and 'staying one step ahead' as per the theme of this chapter. The EA should be aware of what projects are current, their teams, the responsibilities of different members of the team as well as the key deliverables and which team members are responsible for delivering on each of these.

The scope of what an EA might do within a project varies and can be all or a combination of the following:

- a passive team member and observer to report on progress

- an active member of the team, with responsibility for delivering against their own set objectives within the project and to set timeframes

- attending regular project meetings as the representative of the executive, with a remit to provide instructions/directives or to seek information or clarification on specific aspects of the project

- running their own projects.

Even at the simplest level, as an essentially passive observer to ensure they are aware of what is happening and able to report back to the executive, the EA's involvement helps to continue their efforts to keep abreast of everything that may affect the shifting priorities of the executive or changes to the surrounding context.

At the more complex level, where the EA is more actively involved in their own right or acting in the stead of the executive, the EA is able to play a more proactive role. Now the EA is actively keeping the executive removed from a task that he or she doesn't need to be directly involved in, which can only happen when the executive has someone they can trust and rely on to assume their remit and responsibility, and who others know has the executive's trust.

Another interesting element of this is the way EAs can draw on their unique perspective and their broad connections across the organisation to act as change champions. Very recently we heard an example of this in a major professional business services organisation and a project that involved a major office relocation and a move to a more fluid and flexible activity-based working office arrangement. In this case the project was said to have been more successful because the EAs were able to use their connections and influence to help reassure people in the wider organisation, allaying fears about the transition. This was particularly important given the scope of the change. The EAs were better placed – and probably better trusted – than senior management to provide insights into how things would work in practice after the move.

In many ways the project is the perfect circumstance to demonstrate the difference between the 'old' way and the 'new' way when it comes to the EA role. While basic note taking is still useful, the new EA can make a far greater contribution to both the organisation and their executive when they have a more substantial level of involvement in specific projects. The EA's meaningful involvement in projects can contribute significantly to their goal of managing and improving the energy, focus, mindset and relationships of their executive.

Meeting with the executive – keeping abreast of what is influencing their priorities

For every EA we talk to who meets with their executive every morning, or at least touches base with them every day when the executive is travelling, we meet another EA who struggles to have any one-on-one time with their executive in any given week.

This really boils down to a responsibility of the executive. An executive needs to make sure their EA has sufficient access to them if they want them to be able to work proactively and autonomously, playing an active role in prioritising the executive's tasks and activities and representing them through the executive office. This is not time wasted, but rather an investment in time to ensure that the EA can do what they do best in protecting their executive and assisting them to be as effective as possible.

Returning to the topic of shared intent and expectations that I covered in Chapter 2, the need for regular contact – ideally daily at a minimum – should be a commitment jointly made during those early discussions between an executive and their newly appointed EA. We encourage EAs to make this point very firmly. If all else fails, the EA should be proactive in scheduling meetings with their executive. After all, the EA has access to the executive diary and, in an ideal world, should be controlling it.

Several years ago an EA at one of our conferences highlighted the extreme lengths she would go to to accomplish a one-on-one meeting with a her frequently travelling executive. Her tactics included accompanying the executive to the airport in his cab if necessary. This is hardly ideal, but it is a good example of the level of proactivity required of a committed EA who has a good working partnership with their executive and understands the importance of regular communication.

The risk profile of an EA – why they need to sharpen their thinking in relation to risk

When we first launched the Executive Assistant Network in 2005, we were amazed to discover that EAs were among the most risk-averse people in business. The nature of their role and the way they operated, along with the relationship they had with their executive, combined to make the typical executive assistant extremely cautious when it came to taking any action that might lead to them making a mistake.

For instance, we noticed that groups of senior EAs from different organisations who had built strong friendships and support networks with each other often shared very similar supplier lists. When one EA found a supplier that provided the quality of product and service they required, they would share that information with their peers in other organisations, who would often contract the same suppliers without fully considering alternatives. This type of approach extended beyond suppliers. A reliance on the decisions of others was manifested in other projects EAs worked on and in how they were going about their work. We saw it in everything from organising events, functions and parties to how they booked travel and accommodation. We also saw it more broadly in terms of choosing office recycling services and promoting green initiatives, for example.

Now of course relying on recommendations can be a good and efficient way of working – and it is a good way of avoiding risk – but it doesn't always mean you're getting the best deal for your unique situation, which is inevitably different from that of your colleague in another business.

Traditionally EAs have built a reputation for being detail focussed, very considered and particular in anything they did or put forward to their executives. Such perfectionism can be great if you are working with an executive who expects the best of everything that might reflect on their office and on the organisation.

However, perfectionism and risk aversion can hold back the ability of the EA to be proactive. They can be counterproductive. I know that many of those who have self-proclaimed 'perfectionism disease' struggle with this notion, but to work unilaterally and make decisions independent of their executive requires an EA to accept that there will be times when they won't get it right.

I mentioned earlier that many executives need a reasonable level of risk tolerance for the sake of exigency and getting things done. This applies to EAs too. Sometimes an EA has to accept that realising the benefits in time saving for the executive of just getting on with tasks and doing what is needed will require the EA to move outside of their comfort zone and take risk.

Most executives, and even managers and supervisors, who become good at delegating realise that no one is ever likely to do something in the exact way they would do it themselves. However, they accept this as a tolerable situation so they don't have to do everything themselves. It's the result that matters, not the way it is achieved. Such executives accept that sometimes things will not be ideal, but that as long as the risk of any error, mistake or misjudgment can be mitigated to some degree, they are happy to accept it.

EAs need to accept this to an extent and be prepared to discuss such situations with their executives openly. On most occasions we find that executives accept occasional less-than-ideal outcomes when they know that usually their EA does get the right result and that the larger benefit of the EA being proactive outweighs the odd below-par outcome.

As a final note on this topic, there is one aspect of risk taking that I still find unacceptable. You will often hear motivational trainers and conference speakers say something along the lines of, 'Don't ask for permission ... rather beg for forgiveness'. There is no nuance in this statement and, taken at face value, it is simply too cavalier an approach to support a sustainable, trusting EA-executive partnership.

5

Managing information flow and access

AT THIS STAGE IT'S TIME to start getting into some of the nitty-gritty aspects of the role of the new executive assistant. And if there is one traditional part of that role that has somehow remained the same while also – at least in some cases – changing enormously, it must be the management of information flow and access to the executive.

Imagine a spectrum along which EA-executive pairs operate in terms of the management of communication and access. Let's call it the 'information access spectrum'.

At one end of the spectrum the EA is playing the role I've been describing so far, and doing so with the full support of their executive. This EA is fully aware of everything happening in their executive's professional world. They have access to all written communications to and from the executive, including access to the executive's email inbox. The EA has the authority to assess the nature and reason for every request for time with the executive, to make a call on the relative importance of that request and to make a decision on whether or not access will be granted.

At the other end of the spectrum things are very much as they have been for decades, albeit with the involvement of some different technology. In this case the executive cedes little if any control to their EA. They give their assistant minimal access to information flow and requests for access. Their EA has little understanding of their priorities and hardly any scope to manage those they do understand.

In this situation communications flow directly to the executive throughout the day. He or she alone decides what's important and what isn't.

There is no one with the authority to assess these communications, handle them on the executive's behalf or redirect them to someone more appropriate. The EA has neither voice nor authority to play 'gatekeeper' and question those who seek access to the executive. Rather the executive's door – both physical and electronic – is always open to anyone at any time. External requests for meetings may be scheduled by the EA but only after consultation with the executive about whether the meeting should happen and, if so, when it should be held.

At this end of the spectrum the EA is nothing more than a clerical support worker doing tasks assigned to them as and when the executive needs. And while the idea of the open-door policy may seem noble, the reality in cases like this is that the executive is probably constantly stressed, spends hours every day dealing with a mountain of emails, reports and other documents while also managing constant interruptions. Often the EA has no idea what the executive is doing, making it impossible to schedule meetings on their behalf without the risk of a double booking – unless they themselves interrupt the executive.

In our work, my colleagues and I have come across both these extremes and everything in between, though I have to say that we are constantly surprised at how often we come across circumstances very similar to the second 'executive self-management' example. Many executives just don't believe they should allow their EA to see any of their communications, to vet and assess incoming information or to make any decisions in relation to requests for time with the executive.

For executives who work like this, all we can do is try and shed light on a different way and hope they can see that the approach they are using is neither efficient nor effective and is certainly not making the best use of one of their major asset: their EA.

Somewhat surprisingly, it is not the case that the 'hands-on' executive is always an 'old-school' executive who has been doing things this way for his or her whole career. There are also many younger executives who pursue notions of a flatter and less hierarchical management structure in which ready access and open communication are seen as being the overriding imperative, combined perhaps with a belief that modern technology should allow them to self-manage their communications with efficiency. And it is true that so-called 'digital natives', those who have grown up with modern technologies, particularly mobile technologies, know no other way. Remarkably, some of them can even type at a decent speed! However, being able to use technology doesn't preclude the need for an assistant, who can make an executive more efficient by managing access and interruptions, for instance. We rarely if ever see an executive, no matter how modern, who is able to be both entirely self-sufficient and optimally efficient. I will discuss the role of technology further in this chapter.

Other circumstances which affect the EA's ability to manage information flow and access to the executive are newer approaches to office structure. We have seen many organisations moving to activity-based workplaces in which all executives sit at desks out on the office floor alongside other staff. We have also started to see more organisations looking to 'offshore' or 'remote-work' their support teams, including EAs, partly to save money and partly to introduce more flexible working environments. Such arrangements are underpinned by the belief that new technologies make them more feasible. I will address both activity-based working and remote or virtual EAs in Chapter 7.

Prioritisation is all about being able to judge – as demands on the executive shift with the wind – what is the right time to interrupt the executive, given what it is they want to be doing and what they may need to be dealing with at any moment in time. I would argue strongly that the new EA's role in managing priorities and managing the flow of information and access to the executive's office is something that cannot be replaced by technology, nor by virtual or remote alternatives to an assistant in the executive office. This should become clear as I discuss the EA's role in these areas below.

At the end of the chapter I will make a few points directly relating to executive focus, energy, mindset, priorities and relationships to try and enable executives and their EAs to assess what is the best type of working relationship for them and where they should sit on the spectrum I've described in relation to information flow and access.

Executive office triage

As requests for meetings with an executive arrive in the executive office alongside new information, documents, reports and data wanting the executive's attention, EAs often find themselves having to operate a process akin to the triage that is routinely performed in hospital emergency rooms.

Fundamentally the EA's role here isn't very different from the ER nurse's, albeit with perhaps less blood and fewer bandages. The main steps are:

1. Assess the exact nature of each request or piece of information.
This means the person making the request or sending through the information must trust the EA when they seek further information in order to make an assessment, which in turn means the EA needs to have built sufficiently strong

relationships in the wider organisation. This is also precisely the sort of time when the executive needs to have endorsed the EA to perform this 'triage' role and to support their decisions. As soon as an executive starts to circumvent their EA's triage decisions, others will start bypassing the EA and going straight to the executive.

2. Assess who is the correct person to deal with an enquiry or matter and delegate to that person.

Is the executive actually the most appropriate person to handle the enquiry or request? Is there someone better placed to make a speedier assessment and provide a better solution? Can the EA deal with the enquiry or request themselves? If the executive would ultimately delegate the task, that delegation would just as well be done by the EA before it gets to the executive.

3. Prioritise what's left.

Requests that can't be reallocated and information that the EA deems necessary for the executive to see needs to be prioritised. This prioritisation needs to be in line with the EA's assessment and the executive's expectations ... which will have been well established and understood thanks to regular and ongoing executive–EA communication.

Who is the right person to deal with it?

EAs tell us that a significant proportion – often more than 25 per cent according to straw polls we've run – of all requests or enquiries being directed to their executive can usually be better handled by someone else within the organisation ... usually more quickly and with a better outcome.

This is not surprising. It's human nature that staff, customers and others like to have direct access to senior executives and feel they are taking something of importance to them. But of course the reality is that while the executive is probably more than capable of dealing with almost anything that comes directly to them, if someone else is equally or better qualified (and authorised) to deal with that thing, the executive's time would be better spent elsewhere. When the EA acts as a filter in these circumstances, they are directly playing that important role of managing and protecting their executive's time, focus and energy.

Now of course some executives want to occasionally get involved in matters simply to maintain a connection with their teams, to gauge the mood of staff and to maintain a better sense of what is happening 'on the floor'. However, these circumstances would ideally be something that has been planned between the executive and their EA, rather than being the norm.

Is now the best time to bring that up?

On a related note, I remember working with an executive in London many years ago. When someone brought something to her that really didn't need her immediate attention she would use the line: 'If you want an answer on that today then it will be "No", only because I have no time to give it proper detailed time for assessment now'.

This introduces another factor to the EA's 'triage' process: not only knowing when to divert a request but also knowing when to stall it and suggest a better time. At times this will require not only understanding where the executive's focus is at the present time, but also what their mood is. This can obviously be helpful to the team as well, when the EA can give a request a better chance of success – or at least a better chance of getting the executive's full attention – by suggesting the right time to raise it.

Email

One of the biggest complaints we often hear from EAs relates to the issue of having access to and a level of control over the executive's email inbox. We come across scores of EAs who have no access whatsoever to their executive's email. This is something of a paradox, given that before email, opening and managing mail was one of the secretary's main tasks.

When an executive keeps their email private, their EA is not only kept in the dark in relation to a host of issues and concerns, but this ignorance renders the EA effectively inert in their ability to act proactively by, for instance, redirecting an email to someone in a better position to manage it or actually addressing the matter themselves.

In a recent training day we conducted, one EA noted that their executive regularly spent the whole weekend addressing emails that just couldn't be addressed during the week. As a result this executive was gradually getting more and more worn down by the job.

A suggested solution was for the EA to propose a trial period where they categorised emails in three ways so that the executive could assess the EA's ability to more actively assist them in email management. The EA would create three folders:

- one for emails that had been handled or dealt with by a response, or for which a solution had been reached

- a second for emails for which the EA believed they knew what the response or solution should be, and

- a third for those emails that the EA believed the executive needed to deal with in person, or at least provide instructions to the EA on how to respond to them.

The feeling was that adopting this approach would help to build trust, faith and, ultimately, belief from the executive that the EA was indeed capable of sorting emails in this way and dealing with them where appropriate. And of course it would also drastically reduce the executive's email workload and potentially give them back some of their weekend. Over time, as the executive's confidence grew, they would be able to leave the first and second folders for the EA to deal with and only focus on the third.

The reality is that there are hundreds of different methods used by EAs and their executives to manage the email challenge. With many executives wanting to directly communicate with people, it is understandable that they want to be more heavily involved in their email than perhaps they should be from a purely efficiency-focussed perspective. Regardless, we suggest that executives and their EAs need to be conscious of how the approach they use affects the executive's ability to stay abreast of what is happening without being overwhelmed by their email, remain focussed on their key objectives and priorities, maintain their energy and focus, and of course maintain good relationships with key staff and stakeholders.

There is no perfect solution. Each partnership has to use an approach that is right for them. But this is definitely a topic that should be addressed in early discussions about expectations, and then reviewed regularly as part of the communication process for helping to both build and maintain trust.

Meetings and diary management

Earlier I listed meeting and diary management as a basic function of the EA that remains as important today as ever. However, this is another area in which there is a myriad of different approaches and varying levels of EA control, particularly given the advent of the electronic, shared, 'access anywhere, anytime' diary.

In most successful executive-EA partnerships we see, the EA sees maintenance of absolute control over the executive's diary and their schedule as central to their role. It goes without saying that this is essential if the EA is going to play the modern, proactive role I've been describing. Thankfully this is one area in which most executives are willing to relinquish control to their EA.

The bigger challenge seems to be in getting those who want time with the executive to accept that it is the EA they need to make their request to – and to accept the EA's decision with respect to prioritising meetings, suggesting other times to meet, suggesting another form of contact where a meeting isn't really necessary, or redirecting proposals to someone more appropriate.

I'll return to the theme of diary management in the next chapter, this time from the perspective of protecting the executive from others and from themselves.

Reviewing documents and reports

The task of reviewing documents is another in which executives can operate anywhere along the 'information access spectrum'.

At one end of the spectrum we know executives who expect and trust their EA to read and vet all incoming documents and reports before they are forwarded to the executive. In contrast, we also know executives who want to see everything themselves and will not tolerate their EA performing any level of filtering or triage.

For those who prefer to trust their EA with the filtering task, the benefits are often twofold.

First, the EA saves their executive a lot of time when they can identify elements of a document that need work, returning it to the authors for their action. This could be the case where there are issues with the conclusions or supporting evidence in a report, or if the document is not sufficiently addressing the points the executive requested it to address, or if a report is simply badly written and not up to the standard the executive requires.

Clearly, this type of reviewing process can only happen fully where the EA has the requisite knowledge of the subject matter to be able to assess it. However, even for very technical reports an experienced EA will often be able to notice issues that jump out at them, such as formatting, grammar or lack of cohesion. Some of these they may be able to address themselves in a short time.

The second benefit of an EA performing document review relates to their providing some 'protection' to other executives and team members and in so doing building on their relationship with those people. As the person who knows the executive best in terms of what they want and need in the documents they receive, the EA is well placed to provide advice and constructive criticism to others in order that they can meet the executive's expectations before submitting documents and reports, saving everyone a lot of time in the process.

Document review is obviously another topic that needs to be part of the original and ongoing EA-executive discussions about shared intent and expectations. My goal here is not to propose a predetermined way of working, but rather to describe a contextual framework around the role of the EA and how they can help their executive be as effective as possible.

Building trust to support the EA's way of working

I've touched on this a few times now, but it's worth exploring in a little more depth; that is, the notion that for the EA to effectively manage information flow and access they will require the support and buy-in of not only their executive, but also of those who work with the executive. This will likely include managers who report directly to the executive, along with other executives. All these people need to understand why the EA is doing what they do, and how that ultimately makes the executive more effective for everyone.

In this area we move beyond the direct partnership between the EA and the executive – no matter how strong and effective that is – to the partnerships between the executive and those with whom they work.

To restate an earlier point: EAs need to know the nature of enquiries, why someone wants a meeting and what outcome the person requesting the meeting expects to achieve. Only then can the EA properly assess where the proposed meeting sits in terms of their executive's priorities and whether or not there might be a better way to achieve the desired outcome. And if the meeting does go ahead, the EA will be able to effectively brief the executive so he or she can prepare for it.

At one of our recent conferences we discussed this issue in a panel discussion and it was amazing just how many of the EAs said their relationship with the executive's team and with other executives improved once everyone realised and accepted that the EA was their best ally in getting the results they wanted, or at least in getting a fair hearing. However, there was also acknowledgment that getting to this point does take time and something of a 'sales pitch' for a while.

There will be times when the executive needs to show their clear and unequivocal support of their EA. They can do this by reinforcing and educating others in how they choose to work with their EA, and the reasons for and benefits of doing so. They can also do this through their actions – even if this means pointedly not indulging requests that attempt to bypass the EA, such as sneaking in a request over the water cooler. Executives need to prevent attempts to circumvent the EA wherever possible. They should make clear to their team, other managers and executives and key stakeholders that their EA 'holds the keys'.

The flip side of all this is that EAs need to remember that ultimately they report to their executive and, no matter how autonomous and proactive they get, they are still operating at the direction of their boss.

Final thoughts on managing information flow and access

At the start of this chapter I described the 'information access spectrum'. While our work leads us to advocate for EAs being granted more access for the ultimate benefit of executive effectiveness, regardless of where an EA-executive partnership sits on this spectrum it is something that must be discussed and understood. My role is not to tell you what to do but rather to provide a framework, bearing in mind my belief that the new EA's role should centre on proactively managing their executive's energy, focus, mindset, priorities and relationships.

In deciding on the approach to be taken in any circumstances, I believe it is helpful for both EA and executive to consider the management of information flow and access in terms of the following factors.

Managing executive priorities

If the EA is to manage the priorities of their executive in line with clearly understood priorities designed to meet certain objectives, it stands to reason that this extends to the EA managing what information and documents get presented to the executive, and when. It also follows that the EA will manage access to the executive via management of their diary. This will require the requisite knowledge, of course, along with the trust of the executive.

Managing executive energy, focus and mindset

Distractions are frustrating at any time if they are not warranted or needed. Interruptions or requests for attention that don't involve immediate priorities are, by their nature, distractions. So if the EA is to ensure their executive has their mind and focus where it needs to be, as well as the energy and mindset to deal with whatever it is they have prioritised, the EA must have the authority to prevent interruptions, including the authority to make an assessment of the nature of any enquiry, approach or submission.

Managing executive relationships

If the EA has built strong relationships with those who regularly deal with their executive, discussing why an approach or submission is not being prioritised right now should not be a big issue. This will be even more the case where the EA is able to sell the benefits of choosing a better time to approach the issue at hand. Even if the matter is personal, the EA should be best placed to assess the mood and mindset of the executive at any particular time and decide when to bring it to the executive's attention.

There is one caveat to this. Sometimes managing relationships on behalf of their executive will require an EA to tap into to their emotional intelligence and sense when a key relationship for the executive needs to be fortified or nurtured. In these instances the wise thing to do might be to speed things up and set a meeting in the near future, pass forward that document or report more quickly or flag an email for the executive to look at sooner rather than later.

6

Protecting the executive from others (and themselves)

HOW MANY TIMES have we all heard the word 'gatekeeper' used when describing EAs? But ask yourself: how negative is that as a sentiment? What visions does it conjure up in your mind? Probably scenes from movies or television shows of the 1960s and '70s showing a secretary sitting immediately outside their executive's wood-panelled office, acting as a physical barrier to entry – a person everyone must somehow get past if they want to see the boss. Typically this assistant will be a middle-aged woman with a very formal style of dress, a stern look and a generally intimidating presence.

This picture doesn't exactly sit well with the concept of the new EA that I've been describing so far, that of the professional assistant who works alongside their executive, managing their office and priorities and key relationships in partnership with them, to help them be their most effective and most productive. It sits even less well with the notion of the EA being an integral part of the overall team, a facilitator of the best outcomes for both the executive *and* their team.

We touched on executive access to an extent in the last chapter, and clearly there are aspects of what some may see as gatekeeping in amongst that. However, when the EA gets this right, it shouldn't come across as gatekeeping. We prefer to see it as 'protection', which sounds a lot less draconian than gatekeeping. The EA's role needs to include protecting their executive from unnecessary or untimely interruptions to help them maintain their focus and energy in line with their priorities. At times the EA will also have to judiciously decide whether negative office politics, such as rumours or mumblings that might affect the reputation of the executive, are something that the executive needs to be protected from, at least in the short term. The EA needs to be able to decide whether they can deal with such issues personally or they need to be taken to the executive at an appropriate time (which could of course be immediately).

A related role that the new executive assistant often needs to play (and this is something EAs often bring up in our conversations with them) is that of protecting the executive from themselves. This can potentially be confronting for both the executive and their assistant, though in talking to us many self-aware executives have shared their realisation that only their EA is in a position to perform this role.

In this chapter I am going to look at how the new EA can be an effective protector of their executive while avoiding being seen as someone who simply blocks things because they have the power to do so. (I'll discuss the issue of power a little here and return to it in Chapter 10.) The EA needs to remember the importance of the executive's many relationships and manage these in as positive a way as possible, while also at times not being able to give someone what they want immediately.

Protecting the executive from others: the simple time and energy issues

It's a natural human instinct to believe that what is important to us will also be important to everyone else. The person who manages sales sees sales as mission critical, above all other issues. He or she believes everyone else should hold this view, and that any sales challenge should self-evidently be given first priority in the executive mind. But the person who manages production thinks the same of his area, and the person who manages finance sees her problems as pre-eminent as well. And customer service? Well, without customers we don't have a business, do we? None of these areas is fundamentally any more important than the others because none is of any use on its own, but that can be hard to remember when you're buried neck deep in a challenging problem or major project. This is a situation that EAs find themselves confronting all the time. Everyone who wants a piece of the executive's time believes that their issue or need deserves – in fact *requires* – the executive's attention ASAP.

Throughout the early chapters of this book I've often discussed the role the EA has in comprehending and weighing up the competing priorities of their executive, including how various factors might cause a shift in those priorities over time. We've also looked at how difficult it is for an EA to develop the depth of understanding needed to do this well. It's reasonable, then, that those further removed from the executive – including their direct reports – will rarely have a good comprehension of all the executive has on his or her plate. This is precisely why the the EA needs to not only manage their executive's priorities but also manage the expectations of those wanting the executive's time, all the while keeping in mind the natural inclination of everyone to regard their own issues as critical. In other words, it's about replacing old-style gatekeeping with a newer, more conciliatory form of protection or shielding.

And so we return to the need for the EA to be able to build relationships with key stakeholders, other executives, managers and team members to ensure that they understand the EA's role in all this and are willing to trust the EA's judgment in trying to facilitate the best outcomes for everyone. At times the EA will need to be firmer about protecting the executive, perhaps even verging on gatekeeping. At times they will need to be rock hard and completely intransigent. Hopefully this can be done with a level of mutual understanding of the limitations involved and that the EA is only trying to do their job of having their boss's back and helping to keep them functioning at their best – which of course is in everyone's interests.

We'll have a look at this in more detail and examine exactly what it can look like when the EA has to protect the executive from others.

Having the executive's back: looking after their emotional, physical and business wellbeing

As the executive's partner in business, an EA ultimately remains loyal solely to their executive, with the caveat that this loyalty must also be consistent with the best interests of the business (and of course any legal or regulatory requirements). In short, the new EA needs to have their executive's back.

Keeping the world at bay means more than just adhering to the diary and minimising interruptions. It also means being cognisant of an executive's need for sustenance, for breaks, for time to reflect and ponder. It's not just about time management, it's about helping the executive to do what they need to do to maintain themselves at peak physical and mental wellbeing. Only then can they be expected to maintain their energy and focus on the tasks at hand. This will be difficult at times, when disaster strikes or any number of demands make finding a pause difficult. But executives report to us that even scheduling walking meetings or finding other ways to combine space and exercise with work can make a big difference.

Things can get more difficult when it comes to protecting the executive from the cut and thrust of office politics (or even external industry and/

or media attention, depending on the executive's position). Even the most experienced EAs can find it difficult to protect their executive from intentional backstabbing, rumour mongering or other issues that can diminish the executive's reputation and standing. On this, it's a case of prevention being better than cure. EAs need to keep their ear to the ground, making time to get out and about around the office, where they can stay attuned to what is happening and act as something of an early warning system against any brewing storm of disquiet or gossip.

EAs need to remember that protecting their executive from others is vital, and they need to develop the skills to do this without offending others or getting hung-up on internal politics. EAs certainly need to avoid taking sides or politicking themselves, so that they can maintain the strong team cohesion and relationships the executive office depends on in order to function well.

Protecting the executive from themselves

There will always be some executives who baulk at the idea that an EA has a role in sometimes protecting them from themselves. It's perfectly natural that someone who has worked their way into a senior position would feel more than capable of looking after their own wellbeing. Yet we've heard the contrary from literally hundreds of EAs, as well as from dozens of executives themselves.

Some of those executives have shared almost comical – but also serious – stories of their inability to keep a good watch on themselves while also watching their business. We've met executives who admit to getting so caught up in what they are doing that they don't take time for breaks, or even to eat – something that is both bizarre and alarming. No one can expect to operate at their best if they consistently neglect their mental and physical wellbeing to this level.

Other situations can be more significant. I'm going to share a number of examples below, which represent only a tiny fraction of the stories we've heard. I'm sure most executives and EAs will find something they can relate to in these case studies.

1. Focussing on what the executive should do rather than what they want to do

Everyone has those areas of their work that they are really passionate about, into which they love directing their energy and focus. Somehow the things we love to do always find their way to the top of the priority list, regardless of how truly important those things are in comparison with less appealing tasks. In executives this is a trait we see more often in those who have some specific area of technical expertise, usually in the area that they used to work in 'hands on' in the days before they took on managerial responsibilities. Senior pharmaceutical executives with a chemistry background, for instance, or finance executives who started as accountants, or executives in engineering firms. We have seen examples of this in almost any industry.

The underlying problem here is that where the executive can demand all those below them to 'stick to their knitting' without getting side tracked into areas of greater personal interest, there is typically no one, other than a good EA, who can place similar expectations on the executive.

One example of overcoming this challenge that stands out for me involved an EA who was constantly catching her executive working on his area of passion rather than on those tasks that the two of them had agreed were the day's priorities. As the head of a pharmaceutical company who was also a scientist, his personal passion and main strengths lay in research and development, and he was constantly looking to remain more fully engaged in that aspect of his business rather than in the higher-level strategic areas. The EA finally raised this issue with the executive, who agreed it was something that should be addressed. Together they came up with a plan that involved a whiteboard in the executive's office on which the EA would list those tasks the executive had to get done that were a business priority but perhaps not very compelling, such as reviewing reports or reading Board papers. On the other side of the whiteboard the EA listed the tasks the executive would enjoy working on, but which didn't warrant the same level of priority. Both lists were reviewed daily, giving the executive a better sense of how much time he would need to dedicate to the less interesting jobs before turning to those more interesting. The approach led to the executive having more incentive to better manage his time and stay focussed, because this would allow him time to spend on his 'passion projects'. The last I heard, the approach was working very well.

2. Protecting the executive from their own mood fluctuations

Executives are as prone to mood fluctuations as anyone else. They are human after all! Whether due to personal life ups and downs or simply a temperamental character trait, executives can be uneven or inconsistent in the way they approach certain situations and people. Which, of course, can be difficult to handle for those around them, especially those who find themselves the subject of unexpected wrath. Ongoing moodiness can lead to difficult team dynamics, hurt and resentment if not checked.

Often the EA is in the best position to identify issues with their executive that might be affecting their mood. The assistant can also get to know the sorts of triggers that might lead to a negative reaction from the executive. In either case, the EA might be able to protect those in the team – counselling them to keep their distance – or anticipate and reduce the impact of the trigger in the first place. Sometimes more direct action may be needed. We have heard numerous stories from executives who say they rely on their EA to pull them up if their mood and subsequent behaviour is becoming an issue. Getting to this point is a sign that the EA-executive partnership has reached a strong level, based on trust and mutual respect.

At one of our conferences an executive gave me an example of this type of circumstance. She acknowledged herself as a workaholic who was exceptionally passionate about what she was doing in her organisation and the work they were doing for the betterment of the community they served. She told me that there were times when her passion and determination to succeed got the better of her. She could become impatient and exceptionally forceful, angry, aggressive and more than a little short in her dealings with others in the organisation. She was also genuinely concerned that her overreactions and negative comments had the potential to hurt people and cause damage in the team.

'I dread the day when I will lose my current EA', she said. 'She is the only person who can see the warning signs and stop me before anything untoward happens.'

If her EA spotted a shift in the executive's mood, the EA would approach her and tell her that she was on the cusp of 'losing it'. The EA would suggest that the executive physically remove herself to her office and remain there until she was able to bring her passion down a couple of notches. The EA would even find other things for her boss to work on to allow her to regain her composure.

'My EA is the only person who knows when I should be locked in the office', she told me. 'She plays an essential role in protecting me from myself, and by extension protecting the team from the damage I might cause.'

3. Protecting the executive who always wants to please everyone and can't say no

In today's business world, executives are far more attuned to the need to be inclusive, to be part of the team rather than sitting removed from it, and to be as accessible as possible. However, some executives can take this too far, to the point that it becomes detrimental to their own productivity. In trying to please too many people they allow conversations to happen in inappropriate places and often agree to things on the fly, without formalising them in a meeting where they can be addressed in a considered and planned manner.

Now obviously there are times when executives can be inclusive and spontaneous and the outcomes of these situations can be exceptionally positive, engendering greater team bonding, loyalty and respect while also helping to achieve the strategic outcomes and goals everyone is working towards more expediently. But not always. EAs need to have a strategy for handling an executive who is too eager to please too often, and who doesn't know how to say 'No'.

In an EA panel discussion at a recent conference, several of the panellists admitted having worked with executives who would accept any invitation to a meeting or function on the fly, without first checking their schedule with their EA. It often fell to the EA to go back to the person or group who had made the invitation and politely back out of a commitment. As was pointed out, the unintended result of this was often that people were let down, which affected team and stakeholder relationships – difficult situations to manage. Several EAs said that they had been forced to sit down with their executives and explain the consequences of their spur-of-the-moment actions, requesting that they refrain from saying 'Yes' on a whim for no other reason than trying to be nice (as opposed to responding to an unexpected business situation or opportunity). The EAs emphasised that this didn't mean declining requests, but simply redirecting them via the assistant and saving the potential for embarrassment all round. It was pointed out that an additional benefit to this approach was that it made it easy for the executive to decline a meeting if it was something they preferred not to attend, but allowing the EA to deliver the 'bad news'.

4. Protecting the executive who refuses to prioritise workloads or delegate

Striking the right balance between one's working life and personal life is always difficult, and it certainly never gets any easier in today's connected world. The impact of excessive workload on senior executives can be extreme, leading to fatigue, mental health issues and even burnout. EAs can play a role here in managing their executive's energy and focus and maintaining their executive's ability to work at their optimal level. When they have a boss who is prone to working excessively long hours during the week and/or on weekends, they need to work with them to find ways to provide protection and reduce their workload.

Of course there will be times when any senior executive has to put in the hours, such as during a major project or a seasonal peak (tax time in an accounting firm for instance). But these should be the exception, and indeed they can usually be planned for well ahead.

There are also those executives for whom routinely working 12-plus-hour days and working on weekends is a part of their life – those who are driven by their work alone. This may not be something the EA needs to be concerned with, though everyone needs a break sometimes, if only to eat and get some fresh air. And, of course, the rider here is that the executive's ultra commitment to work should not drag the EA into working similarly long hours unless they choose to.

The problems arise when excessive hours have become a way of life not by choice, but rather through the executive's inability to effectively manage their workload, to prioritise effectively, to delegate work to others, or to resource their teams sufficiently. For these people, the extent to which the EA can assist may be minor, though I would suggest that a strong EA-executive partnership should be able to find ways to improve the situation. Simply allowing a competent EA to provide the sort of protection we have been discussing, to play an active role in the management of information flow and access, and in general to perform the role of the *new* executive assistant, will start to make a difference.

We did hear a story from one of our advanced diploma students whose main objective in doing the diploma was to learn how to deal with exactly this type of situation. She desperately wanted to develop greater project management skills and improve her strategic awareness and business acumen so she could take on a more proactive role to assist her executive. However, she was faced with an executive who was reluctant to delegate and cede more control of certain areas of the business to others. After some months, we heard from the EA that she had gradually been able to make some inroads into this reluctance. She was able to help the executive accept that he could offload some of his work to others in the team. There was a way to go: the executive still had concerns about surrounding himself with more qualified and knowledgeable people who could better assist him. But the EA was working hard to keep improving this.

5. Dealing with anxiety and stress

Anxiety and stress can exist for many reasons and affect people in many ways. In the case of executives, they can often go unnoticed by many in the organisation as the executive battles on, trying to keep their personal issues out of the eyes of others in the organisation.

Today we are far more aware of the long-term effects that prolonged periods of stress and anxiety can have on a person. I'm not going to spell out the potentially serious detrimental consequences of this when it affects an executive, not just for the person in question but also potentially for the business. From minor related ailments to major medical issues like heart and blood-pressure problems, anxiety and stress, if left unchecked, can be major concerns with wide-ranging impact.

So what has this got to do with EAs? That is a tricky question. As someone whose role includes looking out for and protecting the executive from themselves, an EA does need to be attuned to these problems and hopefully spot them where they can, without an expectation that the EA will be trained to do so. As for what to do about signs of stress and anxiety, most EAs would be as unqualified as I am to give advice on dealing with their causes and symptoms, but that doesn't mean they can't seek advice to try and help find some form of support or help for their executive or, at the very least, talk to them about their concerns and encourage them to seek professional advice.

Over the years we've had a number of confidential conversations with EAs who have been incredibly concerned about an executive they work with. Some have gone so far as to seek the advice of a medical professional to try and help, followed by the open, honest, frank and very supportive conversations with their executive they felt were needed. Somewhat surprisingly, none has ever told us that these conversations have not been welcomed, probably because they have been instigated by someone they trust and who was coming from a place of caring. Many of the executives in these situations have agreed to seeking further professional advice of their own, with many ultimately taking up meditation and yoga and other remedial steps.

I recognise that this is at the extreme end of the spectrum in terms of what an EA might do to help protect their executive, but it isn't surprising that many executives develop such a strong and mutually supportive relationship with their EA that the EA is able to provide such help. Once again, the EA is probably the only person in the organisation who is placed to do so. And who doesn't need that type of support, no matter where they are within an organisation?

Several years ago, the CEO of a bank in Sydney talked to us about his relationship with his EA. He outlined the nature of the relationship he had developed with her and he confessed openly that she was the only person in the business with whom he could discuss his fears. He cared about his business and all its people, and sometimes the decisions he had to make that would affect those people hit him hard. He truly cherished being able to discuss these issues with his EA. Theirs was one of the truest EA-executive partnerships and relationships we have experienced.

7

From corporate thermometer to the glue in an executive team

The EA as a highly social corporate networker, relationship builder and relationship manager

WALK INTO ANY OFFICE and ask a question about who does what, who has responsibility for what or where things can be found and typically an EA will be on hand with the answer. This isn't because EAs just happen to know stuff. In the case of an effective EA, they know what's going on because they need to. They provide the critical link between the wider organisation and their executive. EAs need to be extremely well networked throughout their organisation, providing frequent and up-to-date feedback to the executive about what is going on and the mood of the organisation. This goes further than being the 'early warning system' I mentioned in the last chapter. It's about helping the executive, who by the nature of their role will often be away from the office, to remain in touch.

In the TV drama *Suits*, the character Donna is assistant to Harvey Spectre, a lawyer in a top-tier firm in New York. Donna is often referred to in articles and conferences as being the epitome of a great EA. Now I'm not necessarily sure this fictitious character demonstrates all the qualities of the new executive assistant I have outlined so far, but with regard to staying on top of what is happening everywhere in the firm and providing crucial feedback to her executive, she exemplifies that trait.

Throughout the show there are endless examples of when she is able to provide information to Harvey and his partners about something she has overheard or witnessed – information that proves critical to their effective running of the firm. Donna demonstrates beautifully how an EA can fill this role in an organisation for their executive.

On one occasion Donna is able to warn Harvey and the lead partner about an imminent internal power move against them. She recalls something another EA told her years before about a suit a junior partner had picked out for the day of his eventual promotion to senior partner. When he turns up wearing that suit, Donna realises he has been secretly promoted by another lead partner in an attempt to gain an advantage in his power struggle against Harvey. It's all very dramatic and perhaps a fair way from (most) real-life situations, but it does serve as a good example of what I'm describing here.

Examples like this are so frequent on the show that Donna has her own catch phrase: 'I'm Donna'. She uses this when people are surprised at some revelation or other she makes about what other people are up to, how they are behaving or something they may have done.

The key to her effectiveness is her ability to network and maintain relationships throughout the organisation. She does this beautifully, even when her executive is struggling with another person only briefly in some relatively minor office-politics situation or legal wrangle. Over and over she works to nurture relationships and, when necessary, advise Harvey when she thinks he needs to take steps to work on a specific relationship, to boost someone who needs it or even just take a step back and let some situation go.

Now, again, this is all fiction. In real life, of course, the type of intelligence Donna manages to accrue is harder to come by – it's not written into the script. But that doesn't take away from the importance of real-world EAs keeping their ears to the ground, maintaining relationships and helping their executive stay in the loop.

Through the rest of this chapter I'm going to look at the EA and their role as a highly networked and connected individual within an organisation. I'll also discuss the idea of the EA as the 'glue' in the executive team, helping to hold the team together at times. This is another area in which the new EA is very different from their counterpart of previous decades, with the new EA getting out from behind the desk much more, in order to devote time and energy to consciously managing team dynamics and stakeholder relationships. It's also an area in which the need for emotional intelligence and social skills – essential traits of the new EA, as discussed earlier – come to the fore.

The final issue we will discuss in this chapter relates those circumstances in which the EA finds it difficult to maintain the sorts of connections and awareness we've been discussing due to the structure of the role or issues of proximity. This can be the case where rationalisation programs have led to a single EA supporting multiple executives or where an EA is allowed, or even encouraged, to work more from home.

The EA as a corporate thermometer

All executives need to be able to test the mood of the organisation at any time with confidence that they know what they are going to find. Whether it is to assess the impact of new policies or strategies, to gain corporate intelligence with regard to performance and success, to gauge how PR and marketing campaigns are truly being felt by people throughout the organisation, or for many other reasons. Executives hate surprises, and effective executives would rather know the truth than what people think they want to know. As such, they need to know what is going on beyond what might be reported by established internal reporting mechanisms.

Good EAs provide this feedback for their executive. They maintain a true sense of what is happening as opposed to what some might want to believe or report. Their gauge of the real mood or culture is often based on their being able to interact at every level throughout the organisation and across all divisions or departments.

The EA as an intelligence gatherer

Aligned to this, but of much more importance in terms of the day-to-day operational aspects of the organisation, the delivery of projects against strategies and the implementation of policies, EAs need to gain intelligence.

In one large professional services firm, an EA told us how she had identified that two different departments under two different partners were running almost identical projects, both looking to achieve almost the same outcomes ... but neither was aware of the other's work. Clearly the cost to the business in wastage of time and resources due to this duplication was huge, and so was something the EA's executive needed to know about. She found out because she was an active participant in the firm's internal EA and PA network and regularly talked with others about what they were focussed on and prioritising.

This level of intelligence gathering can extend well beyond duplication or similar examples of one hand not knowing what another hand is doing. It can be used to understand and relate how people are coping, what people are achieving (or failing to achieve), where internal squabbles are causing issues that need to be dealt with, or even personal staff issues the executive should perhaps be aware of.

Office politics – why great EAs sit above them

Office politics is inevitable in any organisation. It is inevitable where executives are vying for new areas of control, for more resources or for changes in policies or strategic objectives. And it can be extremely detrimental at times. For EAs the challenge is not to ignore or expect to extinguish office politics but to be aware of how the politics is being playing out, and to keep their executive abreast of the manoeuvrings as they happen. The trick is to do this while staying above the politics themselves, not being drawn into them.

EAs tell us that they often have to go to extreme lengths to actively maintain good relationships with everyone in the organisation despite what may be happening at more senior levels above them.

Of course sometimes the politics may involve the executives themselves, which can make staying out of it contradictory for an EA who wants to maintain their loyalty to their boss while also staying above the fray. These situations require a fine balance between being loyal and not actively (or inadvertently) doing something that might hinder their executive in what they are trying to achieve. Much of this normally comes down to keeping confidences, but ideally it should also see the EA keeping their attention on the day-to-day functioning of the executive office, regardless of any storms brewing around them.

Potentially more complex situations are those in which office politics is brewing among junior staff, or even among EAs. In these situations the EA needs to think very carefully about how they should or shouldn't get involved. It's so easy to get personally drawn into these more minor level squabbles. But, again, good EAs do learn to rise above these things, to keep their eye on the brand and reputation issues of the executive office. They also need to make a call about when to keep their executive informed of these more junior wars and when interrupting the executive is really not necessary. If there is an opportunity to use their position to diffuse a situation while remaining professionally distant, this is probably worth consideration.

The elevation of the new EA to a more senior strategic level partnership with their executive has made negotiating office politics at any level somewhat more complex, but that doesn't mean that it should be ignored – that's just a recipe for things to get out of control.

The glue in the executive team

EAs often tell us how they play an active role in helping to manage the relationship the executive has with each of their team members. They often end up also helping to manage the relationships between those team members, especially where the executive doesn't have the best people-management skills, is heavily focussed on some major project, or travels a lot.

If the EA has developed the level of trust and support from those team members I've previously described, wherein the team members accept that the EA has a valid role in helping to manage executive priorities and so on, then the potential for the EA to also maintain relationships within the team on behalf of the executive is easier. Trust and belief are major factors here. The EA who is trusted by the team members will naturally be better placed to not just help in managing those relationships, but actively take on a leadership role in doing so.

To return to *Suits* briefly, this is another area in which the character of Donna is very adept. She plays a skilful game in helping to ensure the relationships between people under Harvey remain positive and professional and does so regularly without recourse to him.

Clearly for this to work the EA must be able to recognise when a situation escalates to the point where it needs to be dealt with by the executive.

There is a more positive aspect to the EA's role as glue in the executive team, and that is the potential to ensure that people in the wider executive team are getting the support they need from the executive. By staying in touch, maintaining strong relationships and understanding the needs of team members, the EA has the ability to bring the executive's influence to bear when it can be helpful, sometimes in situations where team members might have otherwise been reticent to reach out for assistance. Once again, in such an instance, the EA acts as the facilitator of best outcomes for the executive, the executive office and the executive team.

The role of EA as 'glue' is rarely a prescribed one. Ultimately the executive has direct management of those who report to them, but the trusted EA is well placed to reinforce the executive's efforts here and ensure that he or she isn't constantly being drawn into situations between team members if they can be smoothed over without executive involvement. That said, we have come across EAs who do have management of executive team relationships as a formal part of their role, and we have seen the inclusion of performance-measurement criteria – in terms of the executive team's cohesion, stability, happiness and morale – in the EA position description.

Managing key stakeholder and client relationships

Beyond helping the executive to manage relationships within their team, the EA has a similarly important role in helping to maintain relationships with other key stakeholders, both internal and external to the organisation – including, of course, important clients and customers.

The first step to accomplishing this role is knowing who those stakeholders and clients or customers are, and their place in the 'executive world'. Put crudely, how important is each of them? In each case, does the relationship have the potential to negatively or positively affect the world of the executive and the wider organisation, and in what ways?

Doing this takes us back to earlier discussions about shared intent and expectations, and ongoing communication. The EA needs to be regularly brought up to speed with anyone they are likely to interact with, who the executive deems important, and why. In each case, what is the potential impact of this person on the executive and their office?

From a strategic perspective, the EA needs to know how each stakeholder fits into and around the other priorities in the world of the executive, bearing this in mind when they receive a request for information, a request that a document be presented to the executive or a request for an appointment. And as with everything else we've been discussing, the EA also needs to be clear about when they can be proactive in relation to some stakeholder issue without necessarily consulting with their executive in advance, such as a request from an external stakeholder for some piece of information.

With all this knowledge, the EA can go about building a relationship with each of these people as the circumstances allow, uncovering background information including their preferences for meeting and communication. They can also go about establishing good relationships with those around the stakeholder, including their EA or other key staff, knowing very well that it is through these people that they will most likely be able to get things done quickly.

Most EAs know the power of simple things like keeping a diary of important dates their executive should be aware of, such as the birthdays of key stakeholders, who their children are and what is happening in their lives. This is akin to protecting the executive, from the perspective that the EA can and should know what is likely to be important in the minds and lives of the stakeholders, relaying this to the executive and so helping them to maintain their strong connections. From organising regular dinners and simple gifts to invitations to social or formal events, the new EA really needs to be able to pre-empt what their executive would expect in terms of massaging important relationships over time. At times the EA might also need to prompt their boss with a suggestion for some additional 'TLC' when they sense that a relationship needs it.

Avoiding being played

Every EA will know of times when they believe their relationship with their executive has been used by others to try and feed information or gossip through to the executive without the person having to do this directly themselves. People constantly make comments to EAs in the unsaid hope that those comments will filter their way through to the executive without being attached to the speaker. These might be anything from complaints about other staff to more significant issues like workplace bullying or harassment.

It is not uncommon for an EA to be told something 'in confidence' in the hope that that confidence will actually be broken, the EA putting their loyalty to the executive first.

There are times when games like this can be useful for everyone involved, but most of the time an EA needs to know that they are being played and how to push back effectively. This may mean calling out the person bringing the information, dealing with that information on the spot, or simply suggesting that the person take their comments to the executive directly. There are times when an EA needs to be quite forceful in instructing someone to talk to the executive themselves rather than expect someone else to pass their information on.

Again, the EA needs to be able to make a call on what should be brought to the executive's attention versus taking action themselves in a way they know their boss would deal with it anyway. And, again, it's all about managing, protecting and nurturing relationships. It isn't always junior staff who try and play or manipulate the EA in this way: senior managers and junior executives are also capable of playing this game, which can make the politics of the situation more complex.

The keys to building strong internal networks

For some people, building relationships is second nature. It happens without thought or planning. But given how important relationships are to the success of any EA, if relationship building doesn't come naturally they need to have a firm plan for making this happen. I would suggest that even for those who are naturally skilled in this regard, keeping a plan somewhere and checking in with it every now and again is useful.

- Accept that as an EA you need to build and maintain many relationships, and know who these need to be with.

- Actively work on relationships and don't just leave them to chance.

- Try and connect on a personal, albeit professional, level with those within the organisation that you need strong relationships with.

- Keep a chart or plan of people in the organisation, from those who are useful and necessary to those who are vital for formal and informal information gathering, gauging the mood or corporate temperature and/or facilitating projects and getting things done.

- Actively consider your relationship with each of these people on a regular basis and proactively think of any steps you might take to bolster each of them.

- Make it a priority to be visible throughout the different areas of the business as often as possible, maintaining a names-basis relationship with as many people as possible.

- Build strong relationships with all other assistants throughout the organisation. (Formal internal EA networks are very useful in this regard.)

Issues with rationalisation projects, distance working and activity-based working

Let's consider the issues raised in this chapter in the context of some of the trends in office management, namely activity-based working, distance working and rationalisation. In short, where activity-based working, with its open and fluid working style, has the potential to facilitate stronger and more open relationships, I would strongly suggest that distance working, and especially the offshoring of EA roles, makes this virtually impossible.

Activity-based working

Some of the EAs in our network have raised concerns that activity-based working – in which people from different departments locate near each other for the duration of a current project – makes it difficult to keep track of who is who and what department they are from. However, in general activity-based working is seen to be mostly positive in helping to foster strong internal relationships.

That said, from a negative perspective, activity-based working reinforces the issue I mentioned earlier in relation to the EA's ability to manage executive priorities, information flow and access simply because the notion of the executive office is harder to maintain. Without a physical office the whole idea of 'the office of the executive' becomes somewhat redundant, which makes bypassing the EA much easier for those who would seek to do so.

The remote or 'virtual' EA

The circumstance of EAs working remotely, including offshore, is a very different matter to that of activity-based working. When an EA is physically removed from their executive and large parts of the organisation, it makes pretty much every aspect of the new executive assistant almost impossible to achieve.

Remote EAs find it extremely difficult to build active, strong relationships throughout the organisation. They can't effectively act as the glue for the executive team, manage executive relationships, deal with office politics, be the corporate thermometer or gather organisational intelligence. It is almost impossible for a remote EA to be the conduit of information flow and access for their executive, to be proactive in managing their executive's priorities, to be the executive guardian and protector, and so much more.

Many of the things that remote EAs are resigned to doing are the clerical, administrative and support tasks and responsibilities you see on those 'vintage' assistant position descriptions I talked about at the start of this book. A good remote EA might try and add value in other areas, but their task is made so much more difficult without proximity to the executive and to others who are important throughout the business and the executive's team.

Rationalisation of EAs

In recent years we have seen many organisations rationalise EA/PA roles in line with what has happened in so many other areas of business around the world. Principally this occurs because those making rationalisation decisions are focussed on the transactional and task-based elements of the assistant's role and ignore all the potential value-add of the new EA. We have seen extremely large corporations remove up to 50 per cent of their EA workforce, replacing one-to-one EA-executive relationships with arrangements in which a single EA supports a number of executives. Often this leads to the EAs reverting to those basic assistant tasks simply because they no longer have the time or capacity to perform the more complex roles of the new executive assistant.

In Australia we have seen many organisations go down this route only to regret it later, as executives start to realise that their EAs are not providing the additional support and proactively managing their offices in the way they used to be able to. We are hopeful that, among other things, this book will serve as a framework to those considering rationalisation of their EA workforce, or using offshoring or remote working of EAs, so they fully understand the implications of the proposed change.

8

Supporting and promoting executive initiatives and policies

TO THIS POINT I have have talked a lot about the role of the EA in relation to the executive office: the management of information and requests coming into the office and the support provided by the EA to their executive via a broad range of activities and various acts of 'protection' of the executive's focus and time.

But the EA can also, and should, be an active and supportive champion for initiatives or policies emanating from the office, or from the offices of more senior executives.

As individuals who are highly networked throughout the organisation, EAs can play a role in reinforcing the messages the executive wants people to hear at all levels of the organisation. The EA is also in a position – via keeping an ear to the ground – to assess how those messages are being received and provide feedback to their executive. This is obviously of particular importance when a message is not being received positively or not being received as intended.

From office relocations to the adoption of activity-based working environments to mergers and acquisitions to new staff policies – we have heard countless stories of how EAs have assisted in communicating visions, ideas, benefits and much more to other employees, actively advocating and supporting these initiatives.

One example of this was an office move for a multinational firm in Sydney. The relocation to a new national headquarters not only saw a change in location, but also the adoption of activity-based working. In this obviously sensitive situation, the EAs became early advocates of the move. They were actively involved in the project, remaining fully aware of exactly what was happening at the new site, how things were being set up and how things would work once the move had taken place. Feedback we heard at the completion of the project was that the EAs' involvement helped to ensure a smoother transition than would otherwise have occurred. Their ability to counsel other staff, including many executives, by talking to them rationally about the move and explaining exactly how things would work from the moment the move took place, was invaluable. It was the EAs' involvement as much as anything else that reassured people that things would work and operate as planned from day one and that the move would be seamless and easy.

Why EAs?

What is it about EAs that makes them good change champions and advocates for executive communications and initiatives? We have identified a number of factors that we think are worth noting:

- EAs tend to command high levels of trust and respect across all levels in most organisations.

- EAs are recognised as having their fingers on the pulse and being privy to information; they know what is really going on and why, not just what people might be being told.

- EAs are recognised for having high levels of integrity because of the nature of their role and who they work with.

- EAs are seen as connected to the executive teams while at the same time being more 'real' or 'normal' – more like ordinary employees.

- EAs tend to have built trusted relationships throughout an organisation and at all levels, from the mail room to the CEO's office.

Advocacy, integrity and being probed for more information

In many initiatives there will be occasions when staff are by necessity only told part of the story. It's not that executives intentionally want to mislead their staff, but there may be commercially sensitive aspects of any initiative or announcement, for instance. An initiative may be just one part of much larger plans that the executive team is not yet ready to share.

In these situations EAs can feel compromised if they are aware of more details than they are able to share, especially when the internal rumour mills are very active and the corridors are full of speculation. Sadly, this is the nature of the role as the EA straddles those levels that are privy to sensitive information while also having regular contact with those 'out of the loop'. At times this can make the role of remaining a change advocate very confronting. But just as executive teams have to accept this as part of their role, so do EAs.

Some things EAs should keep in mind in these circumstances are as follows:

- They need to adopt a mindset of belief and trust in all executive decisions that are lawful and in the best interests of the organisation.

- They have to remember their loyalty lies with their executives and not with their friends throughout the organisation.

- They have to be very wary of 'wolves in sheep's clothing' probing for information, especially those who might insinuate they are aware of more details than is the case in order to get an EA to divulge information.

- With these points in mind, EAs need to advocate for and support any message, while staying on script and not deviating in order to try and soften a blow or make things more palatable.

- EAs should report back to their executive any specific rumours, complaints or sentiments they witness that are destabilising and at risk of seriously derailing a message. As best they can, they also need to be able to explain what (and who) might be the cause of any confusion and misunderstanding, angst or outright opposition.

- They should be aware that being seen as a spokesperson or a mouthpiece for executive-level decisions and initiatives can affect their ability to remain seen, to some extent, as 'ordinary' people. This can make it harder for them to foster the types of relationships I wrote about in the previous chapter – those needed for EAs to act as corporate thermometers. This usually just means that they need to be aware of when they'll have to work harder at building and maintaining relationships at every level.

9

Networking externally

Building an EA support network and
getting to know important external
organisations and clients
or customers better

THE NEED TO HELP EAs build and develop their networks was a driving force behind the establishment of Executive Assistant Network.

My business partner and I first conceived of the Network in 2005 because of stories we had heard from EAs we knew, and the simple realisation that they needed support. Our goal was to assist EAs to develop their own networks and benefit from the support that comes from being a part of such a network. The education components of the Network were developed later, as we came to understand the overall lack of ongoing training support for executive assistants.

When we started out we knew there were some EAs who had already connected in small but very strong groups of colleagues from other organisations, and that these groups were used for feedback, support and help. EAs who were members of such groups told us how vital it was to be able to speak to people in similar jobs but different organisations. They relished their internal EA connections and networks as well, but it was the external networks that provided the most valuable, independent and unbiased support, along with indispensable information on organisations, potential suppliers, sensitive work-related issues and much more.

External networks with other EAs can provide more strategic business benefits too. Getting to know the EAs of those in your executive's network, or in organisations related to your own, can provide value to both yourself and your executive in terms of meeting your objectives. These types of connections are often, though not always, less personal than the general support ones, but they can be very useful in getting things done.

External EA support networks

We all have occasions where we need information or advice from someone outside our organisation. Senior EAs often report the need to seek such information or advice because they don't want others internally to know what they are working on, don't want others internally to realise that they are not experts or don't have all the answers, or just because they want impartial input uncontaminated by office politics.

Now obviously seeking external input should not be seen as supplanting the need for good internal EA networks. Internal networks provide many other benefits and are heavily relied on by most EAs. However, there are times when an executive assistant just wants to consult with external colleagues in similar situations.

In external networks EAs can often talk in generalities, safe in the knowledge that the person they are talking to will not spend the whole conversation and its aftermath trying to read between the lines to work out what is really going on and/or who is being talked about. When sensitive matters arise – issues with other staff or colleagues, with their executive or relating to specific circumstances they are experiencing – a close friend and/or contact in a similar role, who understands the EA role and what it entails, is the best person to provide support. Of course, to get the benefits of an external network the EA needs to find one to join. For a long time this was difficult. Until we first launched Executive Assistant Network in 2005 there was no other dedicated public group representing just EAs and PAs in Australia. A number of similar groups now also exist in other countries.

Today, of course, external networks are not restricted to people you already know or to face-to-face meetings and conferences. The chat room on the Executive Assistant Network website is heavily used by members seeking external input. They look for advice on venues, restaurants or other suppliers. They share templates, policies and guides. They share ideas about how to approach certain tasks or problems, such as dealing with email inboxes or document sharing. And they discuss new technologies and apps. The chat room also provides the facility for members to chat anonymously if they need to ask more sensitive questions or seek more personal advice. Fundamentally, the chat room provides many of the benefits of the external network, albeit in a different format to face-to-face meetings and conferences. Other public and private groups of EAs also exist on sites like LinkedIn and Facebook.

External EA strategic networks

The strategic potential of external EA networks fits into the broader role of the new executive assistant I have been portraying in this book.

If part of the role of an EA is to work proactively to help the executive achieve their strategic objectives, then just as EAs need to deepen their knowledge about their organisation, how it operates, its strategic objectives and why they exist, they also need to deepen their industry knowledge. They need connections within the industry they are in, with industries and companies that supply it, and with organisations that might have impact from a regulatory, legal or financial perspective.

Being a well-connected EA within your own industry, and with all those external organisations that in some way influence or impact on your organisation, will greatly improve your ability to provide the sort of sophisticated support to your executive that is the domain of the new executive assistant.

A couple of years after we launched Executive Assistant Network, one of the EAs on our advisory committee recounted a story to us about a conversation she had had with her executive, the CEO of a major Australian corporation. Her boss asked her why she was so involved with the Network and was giving so much of her time to it, given how busy she was with the day-to-day aspects of her role. She turned the question on him, listing a number of organisations with whom she had organised meetings for him in the previous year. She pointed out how quickly she had been able to arrange these meetings after he had asked for them, and asked him how he thought that had been able to happen. The main reason, she explained, was that she had at least one good EA connection in every one of the organisations in question. It wasn't always the EA of the person he wanted to meet, but it was someone who could facilitate a quick introduction to the assistant she needed to connect with.

In our experience it is usually easiest for EAs to start by focussing on building strategic networks with other EAs before aiming to build relationships with other players or executives. Those EA connections will quickly provide the potential to facilitate those quick meetings or to share information, providing immediate benefits.

Business development for EAs

At a conference in Melbourne a few years ago, an EA and her executive discussed the extent to which her role had evolved. They recounted how the EA's KPIs had started to include business development as an objective – which certainly stretches the boundaries of even the new EA role as I've been describing it. However, the executive in this instance pointed out that he wanted his assistant to think strategically about the objectives of the organisation. When she was at external events he wanted her to think about what relationships she could foster that could be of strategic importance to the organisation, then document these for the executive to be able to see.

On another occasion we were attending an events industry function and invited some close friends who ran a consultancy in strategic marketing, rewards and loyalty programs to join us. Some of our Network members ended up seated at our table for dinner. One of the EAs was intrigued by this consultancy and the work they did, and in particular by the proprietary technology they had developed for data mining and understanding customer engagement, loyalty, buying habits and much more. The EA realised that what they were describing in terms of technological capabilities was close to what she knew her CEO was seeking for one of their projects. After asking our friends if they would be amenable to meeting with her executive the next day, she set up an appointment on the spot.

This EA acted proactively, without checking first with her executive, because she felt confident that she understood one of the challenges he was trying to overcome. She was also confident that our friends' business would be able to help him achieve his objective. Her actions were a perfect example of what I have been describing throughout this book: the actions of a proactive assistant who shares a strong level of trust with her executive. She had faith that her boss would trust her judgment on this, irrespective of the outcomes of the meeting.

Other EAs have told us stories about how they have helped cement new client relationships, opportunities for expansion and even openings for acquisition through the strong ties they have forged with other organisations.

The new EA needs to be aware that when they are networking or even socialising externally, as a representative of their executive and their office they have the potential to actively influence relationships that could be of significant benefit to their organisation achieving its goals and objectives.

Supplier networks

EAs often have direct purchasing or ordering authority in a vast number of areas, and the ability to influence many more. As they become more involved in project teams and helping with the delivery against strategic objectives, their scope to influence purchasing decisions only gets larger.

I've already mentioned EAs who have told us about their involvement in working on projects including disaster recovery sites, office moves and so on. The areas of potential EA involvement are literally endless, it seems, but in each case there is benefit to be gained by forming strong relationships with relevant suppliers as well as by using external networks as a way of performing background checks on potential suppliers.

Of course there are those areas in which EAs have long had involvement: organising events and functions, dinners and lunches, travel and transport, etc. In these areas EAs need to keep their fingers on the pulse of what is happening so they can make the best decisions or recommendations. Once again external networks come into play here. These networks give EAs access to ideas and intelligence about which companies or people to work with and which to avoid.

The risk-averse EA and suppliers

Earlier I mentioned the risk-averse nature of many EAs and how we encourage them to become a little more tolerant of risk – within reason – to free themselves up to be more proactive. This comment came from our experiences with many assistants in the early years of Executive Assistant Network.

In recognising that many EAs had their own small but very loyal EA support networks, we identified an interesting fact: many of the members of these tightly held groups used the same suppliers for many of the same things, such as florists, limousine companies, caterers and event managers.

What was really happening was that these EAs, whether knowingly or not, were mitigating their exposure to risk through the act of banding together. Obviously a florist who provides service to a number of EAs who they know talk together is going to ensure that they consistently provide good service.

Thus we have another example of the benefits of external networks, no matter their size.

10

The EA-executive relationship

The nuances of the personal
relationship, and finding the right
balance and way of working
together

WHAT I HAVE PROPOSED in this book so far is a model and construct for how the role of the EA can be considered in a more contemporary light – the *new* executive assistant. A significant aspect of this shift includes the way in which an EA and their executive can work together very differently than they might have in the past, predominantly in a way that maximises the value of their partnership.

When it comes to the details of the EA-executive partnership, I can't offer a definitive guide. Every EA and executive partnership is unique and ultimately has to find its own way of working. Partnerships vary not only because of the individuals involved and their personalities, but also because of the nature of the organisation in which they exist, including the industry or government area in which it operates, the role of the executive and its scope, and the management and working styles of both parties. There are numerous other factors.

And there is infinite potential variation in the way an EA and their executive can work together. Earlier I suggested the 'information access spectrum' to describe the range of ways an executive might allow his EA to control information and access. That is just one example. From building trust to setting communication preferences, the boundaries and scope of the role, the extent to which the executive empowers the EA to be proactive and act and work unilaterally, the level to which they allow the EA to manage priorities, communications and access, the extent to which the EA is able to manage team dynamics and broader relationships: there is so much scope in what a partnership can be.

And every partnership will evolve and shift in all of these aspects over time.

There are a few areas I haven't yet touched on that are often raised in our discussions with EAs and executives – areas that can affect the nature of the relationship. They are worth visiting briefly:

- The EA as a sounding board, trusted confident and trusted adviser.

- Power, authority and influence: what should the EA have of each of these?

- Speaking with the voice of the executive.

- Acting on behalf of the executive.

- Should the EA do personal tasks for the executive?

The EA as sounding board, trusted confidant and adviser

You may recall an earlier story I relayed about an executive in the banking industry who told us his EA was the only person he could have conversations with about sensitive business issues and the effect they were having on him and his emotional state of mind. This is a good example of an EA crossing into the extra role of confidant and sounding board for their executive, which can obviously only happen where the EA and executive have developed a sufficiently strong and trusting relationship.

We have had numerous other executives tell us how they appreciate the input, advice and opinions of their EAs on various matters. While typically not relating to highly technical or high-level strategic issues, EAs often make contributions about staffing and team performance, attitude and behaviour, customer relations, PR, marketing and social media, and green or environmental policies.

The question that needs to be asked is why, when executives have strong, experienced teams of specialists around them, would they seek the counsel of their EA who, no matter how smart, likely does not have the same level of academic or business qualifications, technical business knowledge, 'on the ground' experience or, in most cases, practised business acumen.

The answer boils down to how a relationship can evolve between a good EA and their executive, and the bonds that can form. EAs in these situations tend to form the type of relationship with their executive that lets them talk more freely and openly. The EA also tends to know the executive better from a work perspective than anyone else in the business or outside it.

But beneath all that lies one main thing, and that is trust.

Beyond the most technical areas, executives seek support simply by sharing and getting feedback from someone they know is 100 per cent aligned with them, and who unquestionably has their back. They also need to hear from someone who they can trust to tell them the truth – an honest opinion as opposed to 'what I think the boss wants to hear'. Many executives are already surrounded by such people and they rarely need any more.

What does this mean for EAs who find themselves in this position when they may not have been expecting it? Most importantly it means the EA needs to accept the responsibility that comes with being that trusted adviser, and acknowledge the trust and faith that is being put in them. The EA needs to acknowledge the reasons why they are being consulted, understanding their unique position with the executive. And the EA needs to understand the importance of telling it like it is and not being just another 'yes person'.

Aligned to this, the EA needs to take stock of the implications of the executive's realisation that the EA has something important to say. Often we see EAs in this type of position who undervalue themselves, not realising that they actually do have a good understanding of the business, its culture and mood. They do have sufficient business acumen and rational business thinking to back up any opinions they offer.

Reaching this stage in the relationship is a validating experience and I would encourage EAs to treat it as such, while also approaching it soberly, cautiously and with respect. Do your best to offer the advice and opinions your executive needs, drawing on your knowledge, expertise and understanding of the business to do so in the best possible way.

Power, authority and influence

Many levels of power and authority exist inside a business: legitimate or positional power and authority, expertise power, knowledge power, coercive power and relationship power, to name just a few.

It is relatively easy, and not so uncommon, for an EA to get caught up in their close relationship to the positional power of their executive and seek to use it to their own advantage.

What EAs need to accept is that unless they have been delegated real authority, it is unlikely that their position actually comes with much real power or authority. In most cases any delegated power will be restricted to specific areas, such as negotiating with suppliers to put on an event or something similar. The EA's real power comes from building the sorts of relationships I've been describing, both with their executive and with their team, the wider organisation and external stakeholders. With relationships comes influence, a different form of power that in the long run will be much more effective and sustainable for most EAs.

One consideration here is the increased focus on governance in modern organisations. Following various scandals, governance is taken much more seriously than it was even a few years ago. Public organisations need to be more transparent than they once were, and executives and staff at all levels have to be above board in all their dealings – at least in so far as those dealings are presented to the outside world. (I feel sure that deep down most people understand that in most post-industrial and sophisticated economies, corporate governance and executive behaviour remain a long way short of perfect.) For this reason EAs need to take extra care in exercising any delegated power, using it only for the express purpose for which it was granted.

Some years ago I was having a conversation with a group of EAs about this topic of power and authority. One of the EAs told me about a situation in which her CEO, his Board and some other senior executives were offshore at a Board meeting and retreat. During their absence it came to light that the sales director had been involved in serious fraud and this was communicated to the CEO. Authorities had been made aware of the situation and the individual in question was about to be arrested. However, the organisation still needed to take formal steps to remove this person, secure the related data and information and hand certain information over to investigating authorities. In the absence of anyone more senior than the sales director himself, the CEO and Board made the decision to brief the CEO's EA and grant her conditional authority to act in certain ways on their behalf in their absence. All this took place within a few short hours and was extremely stressful for the EA and everyone else involved. Nevertheless, accompanied by a representative from HR, the EA summoned the sales director into a meeting, provided evidence that she was acting on behalf of the CEO and on his authority, and summarily dismissed the director on the spot. Security then escorted him from the meeting and downstairs to be met by waiting authorities.

The EA in question used this story as an example of specific power delegation. She was granted specific and temporary power and she knew this was far beyond any authority she held on a routine day-to-day basis. Normally, her only power was that of influence.

Speaking with the voice of the executive

The notion of speaking with the voice of the executive is closely aligned to the issue of power and authority. It is an area of significant debate among EAs and executives alike.

Some executives are adamant that when the EA issues an email, makes a comment or gives a directive, it should be seen as coming from the executive's office and therefore coming from the executive themselves. Essentially the EA is acting as a proxy for their executive.

Other executives find this idea abhorrent. They expect any communications issued with the authority of, and at the direction of, the executive to clearly state that that is the case.

Depending on the nature of the organisation and its rules and policies, the way this issue is handled rests on internal regulations, irrespective of the executive's preferences. For example, some public-sector organisations and even some private-sector ones have very strict governance rules around such matters.

In other cases it depends on executive preference and to an extent on the nature of the EA-executive relationship that has evolved. What we notice is that the stronger this relationship, and the more that the EA is considered by the wider organisation as the manager of the office of the executive, the more this type of assumed proxy seems to exist. Others start to realise that the EA is an 'extension' of the executive and their office and that the EA's actions are a reflection of the wishes and desires of the executive, even if this is not specifically stated every time.

Acting on behalf of the executive

Taking the concept of the EA speaking on behalf of the executive to the next level is the notion of the EA acting on the executive's behalf. I shared the example earlier of the EA who was delegated authority to do this for a specific circumstance in dealing with a rogue sales director. We are finding cases of this extending a little further than that example, with more day-to-day, ongoing instances of, say, an EA representing their executive at a meeting when the executive feels their own time would be better spent on other matters.

As more and more EAs get involved in projects and committees, we are finding that it is now quite common for an assistant to act as proxy for their executive at meetings, with the authority to act and speak on the executive's behalf in those meetings. This authority only extends so far, with limits usually set on the areas the EA is able to chime in on, such as project milestones or the achievement of certain targets and goals.

As with the other circumstances discussed in this chapter, EAs who find themselves in this position need to remember that they are simply acting as a proxy, that while their executive may give them some leeway to use their judgment in some situations, almost always there will be firm limits on how far that proxy can be stretched. Acting on the executive's behalf should never be seen as a sign that the EA has acquired their own level of positional or legitimate power and authority.

In concluding this discussion of power, authority and influence, I want to emphasise again that it is extremely important that the EA and executive discuss this issue and have a clear mutual understanding of what is right for their specific relationship and way of working together. The worst thing that can happen is that it is left to chance until the EA inadvertently oversteps the mark. In addition, the EA must, as I've mentioned a number of times, continue to build on the relationships they need with the executive's team, as over time this will make the issue of 'power and proxy' much more straightforward and 'natural'.

Having said that, let's remind ourselves once again that the complexity of the EA-executive relationship means that what I've written here can only be considered a framework, rather than a step-by-step guide, for how executives and EAs might work together. As the relationship forms, as trust and belief grow, and as a true partnership starts to evolve, then the nature of this power/authority issue will also change. Frequent review of shared intent and expectations, including the delegation of power, is very important.

The EA and performing personal tasks and activities on behalf of their executive

As the role of the EA has evolved into much more that of a true business associate – a partner in business with their executive rather than the old-fashioned reactive and directed personal assistant – the 'personal assistant' aspects of that traditional role are diminishing.

The expectation that an assistant can be expected to perform menial tasks of a personal nature for their executive – dropping off and picking up laundry, running errands, getting lunches, teas or coffees, buying personal gifts, organising personal events and their personal calendar – is increasingly a thing of the past, as is – thankfully – the notion that a PA is little more than a utility for an executive to use as they deem fit.

While having someone run menial errands for a busy executive makes some sense, it doesn't follow that this should be the domain of the EA.

Today we are seeing a dramatic shift away from this as organisations realise that from the perspectives of corporate governance, workplace health and safety and even workplace and employee insurance, it is inappropriate for company resources to be used to sort out the personal aspects of an executive's life.

Many EAs we know now insist on discussing this aspect of a job at the interview stage, with some being quite explicit that they will not agree to running personal chores for an executive as part of their role.

However, this does not mean that the practice has disappeared completely, and nor is ever likely to. We know many executives who are equally as determined that performing personal tasks is and should remain part of the role their EA.

More often nowadays we see a more commonsense approach, even in those arrangements that are close to the ideal 'manager of the executive office' model I'm espousing here. In a true partnership based on mutual trust and respect, neither side takes advantage of the other, while both realise the need for flexibility when business demands dictate.

In the best partnerships we have seen, there are examples where it has worked both ways. We know a number of executives who are aware of the pressures their EAs are under at times and will offer to grab them a coffee or something to eat if they sense the need. Many executives relish the opportunity to get out and go for a walk to grab a coffee, or to take a trip to the lunch room where they can interact with staff. There are even executives who will drop off their EA's dry cleaning if they are going to do their own – the true role reversal!

On the other hand, there are times when, even if it isn't strictly speaking a part of their role any longer, an EA will jump in and perform a small personal task for their executive in the name of facilitating the executive's effectiveness and maintaining their focus.

My advice here is for both parties to include this as part of the shared intent and expectation discussion. Once again it comes down to communication.

11

Position descriptions and meaningful performance measurement

The problem of inaccurate and misleading EA position descriptions, and establishing appropriate performance measurement criteria

IN THE FIRST CHAPTER of this book I highlighted one of the biggest factors causing ambiguity and confusion about the role of the EA: poor position descriptions (PDs). Far too often, PDs written for EAs fail to fully grasp the complexities of the role and the numerous ways in which the new EA supports their executive. In many cases, existing PDs are completely out of date, describing little more than the simplest routine, everyday tasks that have been performed by personal and executive assistants for decades.

This scarcity of effective PDs was one of the driving factors behind our research for this book, and the ultimate creation of our model for the EA role.

Inaccurate PDs too often contribute to a lack of understanding of the depth of the EA role, which in turn leads to undervaluing of the EA in the organisation, ill-advised rationalisation of the EA role in some organisations, equally ill-advised offshoring of EAs and a general failure to make the most of the potential of the new executive assistant.

My organisation recently developed an educational/training course for EAs, based on our model, aimed at helping EAs and executives to assess their alignment on the nature of the role. One of the reasons why the program is so popular and successful is that there is so much confusion and misunderstanding about the nature of the EA role, its scope, what EAs should and should not be involved with, the fundamental purpose of the role and, of course, boundaries and no-go areas.

To help facilitate this initiative we created a questionnaire for EAs and their executives to fill in before the course. It consists of just under 60 corresponding questions for each, most of which are aligned to our model.

These reviews have confirmed without question the vast difference in outlook and opinion between EAs and their executives, but also between executives in the same organisation and EAs in the same organisation.

But I've probably laboured this point enough now. In this final chapter I want to provide some guidance on how we believe EA position descriptions can be written more accurately, providing greater understanding of the role and increasing the chances of the development of a true partnership between EA and executive. Accurate PDs also assist in the creation of more realistic performance measurement criteria, which make assessment of performance more accurate and provide greater scope for ongoing improvement.

Example position description for the new EA

There are many different ways of creating position descriptions. Every organisation has its own way of approaching the task and, usually, its own templates for laying them out. I'm not going to focus on those issues. Instead I'm going to give an example of a PD for a hypothetical new EA role in a hypothetical business, along with some commentary on why I believe the elements in this PD are important.

(Note that in the example below I have intentionally left out generic elements of PDs such as the location of the job, where they have no general bearing on the points I am trying to make.)

Before we start I want to stress that this is just a hypothetical example. As I've said a number of times, each EA-executive partnership has to develop its own way of working and the EA's position description should reflect that as accurately as possible. Each PD should therefore be different in some ways from both this example and any existing PDs. The elements of the example are provided as a guide, with each section adaptable to your own unique circumstances.

EA Position Description

Position and Function

The executive assistant role exists to provide high-level strategic management support, clerical and business assistance, plus direction and guidance to the executive to support the executive in the achievement of their strategic priorities and business goals and objectives.

Objectives

Taking their lead and overall direction from the executive, the EA is responsible for managing the office of the executive in a way that facilitates the executive being their most productive and effective. Working in partnership with the executive, and working proactively and unilaterally within a framework established with the executive, the EA is also responsible for helping to manage executive energy, focus, mindset, priorities and relationships, and for helping to facilitate the best outcomes for the executive and their team of direct reports.

Organisational Position

The EA reports directly to the executive, and as an integral part of the executive's team will have direct day-to-day involvement with the following positions, key stakeholders and key clients. The EA is responsible for helping to manage relationships with each of these people.

Fill in as needed

Key Responsibilities

- The EA is responsible for helping to manage competing executive time, focus and priorities in line with strategic objectives and short-term goals and objectives, assessing any shift in priorities as appropriate.

- The EA is responsible for building and maintaining strong relationships with all team members, other direct reports, internal executives in other divisions or departments, and internal and external stakeholders and clients necessary for the function of the executive office.

- The EA is responsible for assessing and then managing the flow of information, communications and access to the executive in line with identified and ordered relative priorities.

- The EA is responsible for using their judgment to help protect the executive from unnecessary involvement in day-to-day office management issues, team issues and daily interruptions, therefore enabling the executive to maintain their focus on identified priorities. The EA will manage enquiries unilaterally where possible, or bring them to the attention of the executive at a time appropriate to relative priorities.

- The EA is responsible for helping to provide guidance and support to the executive, ensuring the executive has the time and space they require to maintain their emotional and physical wellbeing.

- By maintaining strong connections throughout the organisation, the EA provides the executive with necessary business intelligence and data, including feedback on the temperature and mood within the team and organisation.

- The EA supports initiatives emanating from the office of the executive, or elsewhere in the organisation, as required and acts as an advocate or change champion as required.

- The EA is responsible for building strong networks externally that help to support the executive in achieving their business objectives.

- The EA is responsible for taking on the management of key projects on behalf of the executive and their team, or being involved as a project team member – permanently or on an ad hoc basis as required by the executive and their team.

Main Duties and Tasks

- Manage the meetings and tasks schedules and diary for the executive in line with identified and understood priorities.

- Review all communications to the executive and handle, reassign or prioritise these for the executive in line with identified and understood priorities and areas of responsibility with the team and business.

- Review all submissions to the executive and assess for clarity, style, purpose or objective, and intended or desired outcomes. Edit or request further clarification or edits from the author, and submit to the executive when ready, annotated as appropriate in line with goals, targets or objectives and prioritised for assessment.

- Arrange meetings with the executive in line with understood and known priorities.

- Book and arrange travel and accommodation in line with known and understood needs, priorities and objectives.

- Conduct research for executive and team initiatives or projects as directed by the executive or proactively, based on an understanding of known and understood project or task objectives.

- Draft communications, documents or presentations as directed by the executive or proactively, based on an understanding of known and understood project or task objectives. Present such communications for review by the executive or distribute unilaterally, depending on an understanding of the desires and needs of the executive.

- Plan and organise appropriate meetings, events, functions, dinners, conferences and training as required by the business, with clearly identified objectives in line with known objectives or in line with executive directions.

- Manage and oversee projects as directed by the executive, including the development of plans for such projects based on desired outcomes and approved budgets.

- Participate in projects as a team member with set responsibilities and objectives as directed by the executive.

- Research, source and engage all suppliers with products or services required by the executive office to meet company objectives in line with company policies and spending parameters and budgets.

- Create, develop and maintain strong relationships with all internal and external stakeholders and all clients.

- Participate in and contribute to team meetings and take notes or minutes as required.

- Build and maintain strong relationships with staff and executives throughout the organisation who can support the projects and initiatives of the executive and their team or provide intelligence, data, feedback on the corporate mood, etc., as needed by the executive.

Key Skills and Abilities

- The EA must be an excellent communicator, rapport and relationship builder, with very high emotional intelligence and the ability to maintain and nurture key relationships.

- The EA must be highly competent at managing workflow, priorities, diaries and schedules for multiple persons, including themselves and the executive.

- The EA must have integrity that is beyond reproach and be able to keep confidences and corporate confidentiality without question.

- The EA must be good at assessing and analysing vast quantities of data, information and communications and assessing the relevance of these and their level of priority for the executive at all times.

- The EA must have strong business acumen and business management knowledge and the ability to quickly learn and understand the nuances of different industries and different organisational departments or divisions.

- The EA must be adept at quickly learning and understanding the roles and responsibilities of the executive and their team and others within the organisation who support the initiatives of the executive or have an impact on these.

- The EA must also possess advanced office software skills; strong written communication skills, including the drafting and editing of high-level documents; a strong financial numeracy and corporate finance understanding; and advanced presentation preparation and design skills.

- The EA must be an adaptable manager and leader who can engender support for the adoption of ideas and practices, policies and procedures. The EA must be someone others believe is genuinely working in the best interests of the executive, their team and the organisation.

- The EA must be a strong rational and strategic thinker with well-developed problem-solving capabilities.

- The EA must be adept at dealing with difficult people and difficult situations and at managing and overcoming conflict.

Position description elements and commentary

Following are some notes on the various sections of the hypothetical PD.

1. Position and Function

Setting the tone and purpose for the EA role and giving it relevance at a strategic level is important for ensuring that the EA, the executive and others in the organisation understand the true purpose of the role and what it exists to achieve on a macro level. This section emphasises the point that the new EA role is not just about clerical support, but rather is about providing high-level, strategically important assistance.

2. Objectives

This is an extension of the purpose and refines the way the EA-executive relationship will function and what is expected in terms of the evolution of this relationship into a partnership. It describes areas the EA will assist in managing, still on a macro level, but particularly the aspect that they are expected to work to benefit the executive and their team.

3. Organisational Position

The Organisational Position section reinforces the aspect of the position of the EA in the executive's team and the need for the EA to help manage relationships. It reinforces the EA's importance in building and maintaining these relationships with others, the executive's direct reports in particular.

4. Key Responsibilities

This is the vital section in helping to move perceptions of the role of the EA away from its being predominantly clerical. The section introduces the many other areas the new EA helps to manage and take responsibility for, as well as the ways in which they are expected to help support the executive and how they can do this to ensure the executive can achieve their goals and objectives.

5. Main Duties and Tasks

This gives examples of the many day-to-day tasks that EAs take on, but ties back to the areas of responsibility and describes what the basics of the role are.

6. Key Skills and Abilities

These are the foundations for the EA's ability to achieve all their objectives, manage and deliver against their key areas of responsibility and perform and execute their tasks and duties.

Performance measurement

Performance measurement is essential for a number of reasons.

Having clearly and mutually understood performance measures is an important component of the mechanisms of trust building between an EA and their executive. But performance measures also play a role in helping businesses to understand exactly how their EAs are contributing to the achievement of organisational goals and objectives.

The simple calculation often used for the justification of an EA salary is what percentage of the executive's time is being saved by having an EA perform tasks that the executive would otherwise have to do themselves. The corresponding salary differential means that it is much more appropriate to have someone on a lower salary take on these types of things. A more appropriate approach might be to focus on those things an executive would not have time to achieve were they to be constantly distracted by having to spend time and energy dealing with interruptions or spending time on trivial matters.

However, as I've shown throughout this book, the new EA can contribute in so many ways that go far beyond simple time savings. They can proactively help the executive achieve their goals and objectives for the business by taking on projects of their own, drafting papers, analysing and prioritising communications, strengthening internal and external relationships, providing intelligence and feedback from within the organisation, and in numerous other ways in keeping with maintaining a strong EA-executive partnership, and using the abilities of a talented, knowledgeable and highly skilled EA.

It's always going to be difficult to put a simple number on the value of this contribution. In addition, applying such a number risks creating the impression of precision where there is none.

However, for argument's sake, let's say that in addition to the time-saving aspects of the traditional EA components of the role, a highly competent EA's contribution adds up to a 20 per cent improvement in the executive's efficiency. So if we were to take a CEO earning $500,000 a year, the value of that improvement in terms of the executive salary would be $100,000. This can then be factored against the cost of employing the assistant.

However, what about the impact of the more efficient executive (and in fact that of the new EA) on the wider organisation? Let's say the organisation in our example turns over $300 million per year and delivers profit of $40 million. What would the impact to that organisation be if the CEO and the other executives and senior managers all gained an additional 20 per cent of productivity and output from their respective EAs?

It quickly becomes clear that simple salary trade-off calculations in respect of some executive efficiency gains don't tell the full story. In the example given, even if the overall benefit to the organisation from each of the senior executives and managers having a 20 per cent increase in performance was only a 10 per cent increase in the overall performance of the business, that could still equate to an increase of $2 million in profit – substantially above the cost of the EAs.

Of course, it is possible to hypothesise that increases in output and performance at the top end of an organisation, and therefore greater focus on strategy and performance by those executives, would have an amplifying effect on the organisation as a whole. In other words, that 20 per cent increase in executive productivity may lead to, say, a 30 per cent improvement in turnover and profit.

But of course all these numbers are entirely hypothetical and the problem persists that it is almost impossible to calculate the true benefit to the organisation of a great EA (or any other outstanding employee, for that matter). My organisation has been working on some matrices with an external consultancy to see if we can help shed further light on this matter, and hope to be able to create and publish some of these in the future.

In the meantime, we think it is important that organisations do the following. Regardless of the numerical benefits, these steps will provide real enhancement to the benefits the business gains from its EAs.

1. Have meaningful position descriptions for all EA staff that accurately reflect what they do and the overall strategic importance of their roles.

2. Invest time in trying to instil ways of working between EAs and executives that can deliver the best possible outcomes, within a true partnership, and that focus on the sorts of 'big picture' aspects I have described in this book (and on much more than the notion of simply saving time for the executive).

3. Ensure EAs have adequate skills, knowledge and abilities, both technical and social, to be able to work the way the organisation and each executive needs them to.

4. Implement EA performance evaluation criteria and methodologies that look beyond the achievement of the traditional tasks of the personal assistant – the tasks that are still listed in most EA position descriptions today – and instead incorporate the many intangible elements we have outlined.

5. Align EA performance and evaluation criteria in some way with the KPIs of the executive they work with, enabling a level of direct assessment of the extent to which the EA is supporting the executive in achieving their goals.

In the remainder of this chapter I will focus on points 4 and 5.

EA performance measurement – the basics and the intangibles

Most of the KPIs applied to EAs are still, in our experience, heavily weighted towards basic tasks and duties. We can level the same criticism at these as we do at those outdated PDs. They are generally simple 'yes' and 'no' tick-a-box affairs with the EA assessed as either constantly performing the required tasks ... or not. They are either adept at booking travel adequately to meet the executive's needs, in line with policies and procedures and without errors being made, or they are not. Likewise for organising meetings and events or even seeking suppliers or whatever it might be.

One of the reasons why both EA position descriptions and appraisals stubbornly remain this way is that it makes them simple to assess. And of course all these things do remain a part of the EA role and should be assessed as such. There is no point having an awesome EA who is great at helping the executive in a myriad of more strategically important aspects if they can't get the basics right.

Some of the areas that commonly fit into this category of the basics include:

1. *Diary management* – ensuring the executive's diary is accurate, well maintained and coordinated, featuring all meetings, travel and actions, and researching and planning other times as needed.

2. *Travel management* – ensuring that the executive's travel plans are booked accurately and with enough time built in to ensure they can function adequately in their role.

3. *Managing emails and communications* – ensuring that all emails are dealt with and managed and/or responded to by the executive or the EA as necessary, and filed as appropriate for both the executive and the EA.

4. *Reviewing documents* – ensuring that all documents are adequately

reviewed, proofed and edited or sent back for revision prior to being sent to the executive.

5. *Event management* – ensuring all events, from dinners to functions or educational forums, are adequately planned, resourced and occur without glitch or hiccup.

6. *Project management* – ensuring that all projects are well planned, resourced, and managed throughout their duration, and are executed on time and on budget.

7. *Supplier management* – ensuring that all suppliers within the scope of the EA role in managing the executive office are selected in line with company policy in relation to identified needs and deliver appropriate levels of service in relation to product or service, needs or benefits and value.

8. *Stakeholder management* – ensuring that strong relationships with all internal and external stakeholders are developed and maintained.

9. *Data and knowledge management* – ensuring that accurate documents, files and other records required by the executive and the executive team are maintained and stored in such a way as to be accessible to all those who need them.

10. *Corporate action plan* – ensuring that a timetable or plan of all business activities, meetings and executive team functions has been created and considers objectives, KPIs, the operating process and the reporting process.

But, again, these are just the basics – the same essentials any junior to mid-level assistant would expect to be adept at. They by no means tell the whole story.

In addition to the basics, I propose that EAs should also be assessed against the many other aspects of the role we have outlined in this book.

The starting point of this is that the issue of PDs is addressed, as I discussed earlier in this chapter – consistent, of course, with the unique requirements of the position and the organisation.

As the aspects of the EA role we are discussing here are less tangible than the 'basics', it is more difficult to measure them quantitatively. However, that doesn't rule out assessing them. One simple starting point for organisations would be to have EA evaluations look at some of the areas covered in the EA-executive questionnaire I mentioned at the start of this chapter, and have the executive subjectively rate the EA in terms of how they believe they deliver against those areas.

Some examples are listed below.

The idea is that the executive rates the EA against each from *Strongly Agree* through to *Strongly Disagree* – or whatever scale an organisation chooses to use.

1. Your EA has created or reinforced a personal brand that is congruent with your office.

2. Your EA has helped create a brand for your office that is identified with being trustworthy, consistent, and reliable.

3. Your EA has developed strong internal networks with all important individual or group stakeholders and other teams and divisions, but most importantly with your direct reports.

4. Your EA has acted as an essential corporate thermometer for you, providing you with invaluable information on vibe, mood or cultural shifts in general, or in regard to specific issues or policies.

5. Your EA has provided you with important and useful specific business intelligence, information, data or reports proactively, without request.

6. Your EA has developed their corporate and industry knowledge, business acumen and an intuitive business brain to enable them to fully understand your short-, medium-, and longer-term goals and priorities.

7. Your EA has demonstrated an understanding of your relative priorities and goals in proactively applying appropriate filters to their role as the conduit of information flow and access to your office.

8. Your EA has helped manage your activities and focus proactively, in line with their understanding of relative priorities and goals.

9. Your EA has built and maintained strong relationships with your team and direct reports that has enabled the EA to coordinate team requests, team meetings, team submissions and team interaction with you in a positive manner, while still enabling you to focus on relative priorities as required.

10. Your EA has helped to manage and run projects, or oversee and report on elements of them, with your team or other divisions or areas of the business that have alleviated the need for your time and focus to be used on every aspect of the projects.

11. Your EA has acted as a protector or even gatekeeper to isolate you, in an appropriate manner, from destabilising or distracting influences when required.

12. Your EA has assisted you in monitoring and maintaining your emotional and physical wellbeing and provided support for you to do this as needed.

13. Your EA has acted as a sounding board or provided advice or counsel for you when required.

14. Your EA has proactively helped to manage the smooth dissemination of information, ideas or policies emanating from your office.

15. Your EA has championed and advocated ideas or policies emanating from your office.

16. Your EA has established strong external networks that have facilitated achievement of your business development goals and objectives.

Linking to executive KPIs

Using the measures of EA performance I have listed so far would go a long way towards identifying the extent of an EA's effectiveness as a new assistant. That is, the extent to which they assist the executive to focus on their strategic objectives, manage the executive office and facilitate the achievement of goals and objectives.

What these measures don't do is tie the EA's performance directly to that of the executive; that is, to the executive's KPIs. Ultimately, if maximising executive performance is the raison d'être of the EA, which is what I'm proposing, then shouldn't the EA have their performance measurement related in some way to that of the executive?

Below is a list of common executive measurement areas – it is clearly not an exhaustive list but is used to provide some examples.

- revenue versus forecast
- growth rates

- progress relative to targets
- profit margin
- costs or expenses trends
- net promoter score/customer satisfaction/customer loyalty
- employee engagement.

At the very least EAs need to know exactly how their executive's performance is being assessed. Throughout this book I have stated that EAs need to be aware of strategic objectives and the goals and plans of the executive in order for them to provide assistance proactively. Being aware of what measures the executive is tracking in terms of their own performance targets is central to this, because those measures obviously tie in closely to the executive's overall strategies and plans.

So can EAs be directly assessed against how much they help the executive achieve his or her own targets? It will never be straightforward, but EAs can certainly be measured against what they know and understand of their executive's goals, what they actively do to assist the executive with ideas, plans or initiatives to meet those goals, and how they help the executive track and monitor those goals.

As there is, again, a degree of intangibility here, a potential place to start would be to use a simple system asking the executive to rate the EA in terms of demonstrating their understanding of their KPIs, whether they come up with any ideas or initiatives to implement in respect of them and, of course, what they do to help the executive monitor and track statistics or measures for each of these.

While this isn't a very sophisticated methodology, it would be a start, in addition to the assessment of the other intangibles listed earlier. If nothing else, it would prompt a conversation around these areas, and the potential for the EA and executive to reassess their shared intent and expectations. It would also help to reinforce for the executive the real value they are gaining from their EA.

My organisation will continue to develop methods for assessing the value a new executive assistant can deliver, including via the matrices I mentioned earlier. We have another project that will be looking at how EA performance measurement criteria and processes can be made more robust and useful to the organisation and the executive. These will not be easy to nail down and are unlikely to be simple, given the complexity of the new EA role. In the meantime, what I've offered above will hopefully provide a more useful and meaningful approach to EA assessment than what currently exists in most organisations.

EAs are valuable. But their value can be so much greater with the right approaches, with the right training and education, with the right frameworks and ways of working, and with a better understanding of how they can assist their executives. That is what this book has been for – and I trust it has been useful.

Appendix

Contributions from working executive assistants and executives

AS I WAS WRITING this book I sought out the views of some members of the Executive Assistant Network, as these are the people 'on the ground' who are working in roles of the type described in this book. My aim was to reinforce the main concepts in the book and emphasise the central point, that the role of the new EA is so much more than what we tend to see in most position descriptions.

I received a number of contributions from EAs working in a variety of environments, and I thank each of them for making the effort to put a submission together.

To make the contributions as relevant as possible, I have taken the liberty of dividing them into extracts under headings corresponding roughly with the main themes of the book. Each extract includes the initials of the contributor(s) and a full list of contributors is included at the end of this appendix.

Trust

If you have hired an EA who is happy to just manage your calendar and process your expenses, then news flash: he or she is not a true EA. A true EA who realises they have a boss who just wants them to manage their calendar and collate their work papers will soon be looking for another job.

Today's EAs do not suffer fools lightly. They identify them quickly and tolerate their behaviour only as the job requirements make it necessary. This includes the key executive they are working with. Executive assistants want to promote the performance of their manager, not make excuses for the performance of that manager. (LV)

I believe one of the most important skills required to be a good EA is building trusted working relationships. The relationship between the EA and their executive must be strong, professional and built on trust and understanding. There must be a cultural fit and complementary working styles in order to have a pleasant relationship and get the job done efficiently.

I have found by sharing the same work ethics and morals with my executive that it helps me to be engaged at work, productive and wanting to come to work each day to provide support and achieve outcomes. (NJ)

I applied for a job at a large professional services firm at a time when they started to focus on 'soft skills' within the business. I interviewed to work with a partner who was technically brilliant, however was an introvert and lacked 'people skills'. As I had extensive experience in the service industry, he hired me, knowing this was an area I could assist him with. Trust was built very quickly as he shared his vulnerability with me and we set about making small changes in the 'way we worked'. After a few months, he was able to listen and collaborate better with colleagues, was having spontaneous conversations with staff, understood the intricacies of customer service rather than just delivering a product and was understanding, patient and empathic with junior consultants. We were very different people, yet we shared the same values and beliefs and he knew I had his back whenever he wanted to step outside his comfort zone. I believe this had an enormous impact on both his daily working life and his long-term career. (MLJ)

When you ask most successful EA-CEO partnerships what the elements to their success are, it usually comes down to a series of intangibles that are hard to pinpoint. There is one constant though, and if you're lucky, you'll find it maybe once in your career – we refer to it as 'magic'. When the magic is there, it is evidence of trust, respect, understanding and loyalty. (JW)

Communication

Communication is paramount. I meet with my executive on a daily basis to understand the fast approaching priorities and how best to deal with them. We go over the calendar on a daily basis and move meetings to juggle other commitments so the priorities are met. Emails are flagged as follow-ups well before deadlines so my executive and I are well and truly on top of tasks, which allows us to rearrange the calendar to fit in any last-minute meetings with stakeholders. (MJ)

In our fast-moving, fast-growing company, keeping abreast of the evolving corporate priorities is vital to supporting my executive. We have worked together to define a list of checks that I can carry out on his behalf, which enables him to free up his time for important decisions and opportunities. However, because of our high rate of growth, this list is always changing. (JP)

Communication and shared expectations are key to providing effective support and are the basis for building/maintaining an ongoing partnership with the Executive. You also need to take the initiative in being inquisitive to ensure you know what you need to know. For example, having daily catch-ups first thing each morning either face-to-face on via phone are essential in aligning our focus; sharing priorities; and to zero in on requirements. Being on the 'same page' ensures we are working cohesively. (HC)

Relationships

It's important for the EA to understand and get to know their executive's direct reports and where their roles fit within the organisation. This allows the EA to prioritise meetings or phone calls according to their priorities, ensuring that the executive does not become a bottleneck. The executive might think that one thing is the most important, while not realising the knock-on effects of neglecting something else which, to the executive, seems trivial. (YP)

A significant aspect of my role is to support my executive, the CEO, through the transition (from founder-led company in which the executive was involved in every aspect to a more strategic role as the business grows quickly). The challenge for an EA in this situation is that you need to support not just your executive but the rest of the senior team too. It is my role to work closely with the CEO and the executive directors to help the wider organisation to understand which responsibilities the CEO continues to hold and which have been devolved to his senior leadership team. (JP & IA)

Managing the office

In the modern EA role, the need for EAs to be proactive is extremely important. These days, specifically with the rise of the millennial executive, EAs find themselves working with people who have started out doing everything for themselves. This means that increasingly you are getting EAs being expected to be more like business partners than typical EAs or PAs of the past. In addition, the increasing availability of apps and software that help streamline processes means EAs have more time to be proactive than they had before. Nowadays EAs are developing strategies for social media, or project managing other members of the team so that they can report back to the executive.

When the EA really understands their executive and what their goals and objectives are, they can do a lot more to help them than just managing their diary. I've worked for an executive where most of his team worked on another floor in the building. I arranged weekly 'walkabouts' for him so that he could visit this other floor and people could approach him and talk to him if they needed to. (YP)

As the EA of a CEO going through a funding round, I needed to provide flexibility for my executive by adjusting all his regular appointments so that he could adapt to a rapidly shifting situation. By attending the Board meetings and weekly executive meetings, and by staying in close contact with his direct reports, I was able to foresee a number of the changes to the CEO's diary that would need to take place, and make those changes as the developments were unfolding right there in the meetings. (JP & IA)

I see my role as a facilitator rather than a manager of the executive office where my preparation and performance provides the right platform for working in partnership. I am an advocate of the 'proactive' approach in all that I do. This mindset underpins my approach and ensures my focus is on being productive and effective. (HC)

There is only so much my manager and I can achieve in our day, and with that comes the responsibility to manage the delegation of certain tasks to my team, on behalf of my manager – up or down. Delegation is important for keeping up with the workload without feeling overwhelmed at any time.

It's important that I determine when delegation is most appropriate. I need to be sure that the person I'm delegating to has the necessary information and expertise to complete the task without wasting anyone else's time and perhaps delaying other tasks. I ensure they clearly understand what needs to be done and make them feel comfortable to come to me with questions. Because I work so closely with my team and have a bird's-eye view of what experience, knowledge and skills they all have, I generally understand who to delegate to. (MR)

At Prime Media, Michelle had responsibility for a number of areas within the business and took personal ownership of many projects. One such project was the implementation of a new travel provider for the national business. She collaborated with internal stakeholders regarding their needs, liaised with the provider to complete the Service Level Agreement, wrote the company travel policy, established data for the build, managed the 'go live' requirements, produced training documents and then travelled to capital cities to demonstrate the system. She also sent out a newsletter on how we were tracking against budget, tickets on hold and general travel news. This was a successful and positive rollout across the network and a cost saving for the business as a result of online usage and adherence to the policy. (JPa)

Breadth of knowledge

With the need to be more proactive also comes the need to gain more knowledge and understanding of the business. Having worked at my company almost from when it started, I have learned each job function as it was created. I sit in on most management meetings, and I understand what the company does, and where it is going. I also understand the background to a lot of the decisions that we have made over the past couple of years. It is this which has resulted in me being asked to identify and improve one of the main processes within the business. I have been tasked with looking at the end-to-end process of our core business, and streamlining it to make it more scalable as the business grows. It's a fundamental role within the organisation, and one which an external person would have struggled with initially while they learned what everyone in the company does and how they all fit together. (YP)

My role in the Telecommunications Group Strategy is to support the general manager and group managers to facilitate the delivery of the Group's government directives and initiatives. In addition, to deliver any improvements, leadership and guidance to the Group to support this strategy. I play an important strategic role by:

- knowing what the strategic direction is and how we are going to achieve it

- having insight, by being an active participant, into what outputs staff are delivering over a specific period of time, which in turn ensures I am aware of the Telecommunications Group priorities

- organising and planning the office of the general manager to ensure alignment of the strategic and business priorities. This helps us to filter out the 'noise' and ensure we focus on the key items

- scanning for environmental triggers, issues and 'moments of joy' both internally and externally so that I can bring these to my general manager. This includes noticing potential conflicts within the teams, studies on particular topics and media reports that may be cropping up relating to the Telecommunications Group

- being the missing link. As the executive assistant I have access to various organisational information, which makes me a valuable player strategically. I'm the link who can point my colleagues in the right direction when they aren't sure who to talk to when a specific issue arises; and

- acting as the glue: bringing senior management together to ensure they stay focussed and provide independent advice. I can maintain a '20,000 foot' view of what's happening in the team as I am not tied down in the operational issues.

The progression of this executive assistant role now includes role-related leadership, the management of people, relationships, projects and teams. This must continue to provide the necessary support to deliver the initiatives and it's important that this role continues to actually *be* the position, not just fill it. (MR)

People sometimes underestimate the role of the EA and they do this to their detriment. I see Maria as a critical part of the team, providing the support, advice and direction that ensures that the team can continue to deliver and meet its objectives.' (BM)

I was once in a meeting with senior management discussing processes and revenues. I was meant to be taking minutes, but since I already knew several people in the room from working with them at previous companies, I felt that our relationships were strong enough for me to pipe up and give my opinions too. At one point in the meeting I spoke up and suggested a new revenue stream for the company. After a discussion around the table, it was agreed that we would look to implement it, and I ran with the project until it was handed over completely to our IT team to build and test it. I continued to push for its development throughout the project, even when other things looked like they would overtake my project in terms of priority. My project has just been launched and has proven to be revenue generating already. (YP)

Managing information flow

Over time you get a feel for issues that don't need to go past your executive. Summaries for Board reporting I redirect to the appropriate managers. I can now write up the routine Board paper on behalf of my executive as I've become used to the correct format to follow. (MJ)

I see myself as being somewhat in charge of the success and day-to-day running of my team and to some degree have a lot of empowerment and authority to do that. I consider myself the one who is going to make things happen, I call the play. I think it's important to get involved in the business of my team to achieve this. I achieve that by trying to read everything my manager needs to read. I review all his emails, not just sift through them. I listen to everything he is saying and take it all in. I try to understand what he is involved in and what my team is involved in. I roll my sleeves up and get in on the game. (MR)

I think it's imperative that for us to succeed as a team, Maria and I are both on the same page with what is happening. For this to happen Maria has to read all my emails and my reading so that she is aware and across the issues that are being faced. (BM)

EAs often become aware of information or knowledge that could be important for the executive to be aware of, either of a personal or business nature. Sharing this information may assist the executive in preparing for discussions or meeting so they are 'in the know' and not caught off guard. Of course, there may be sensitivities involved that need to be carefully evaluated. (HC)

By having oversight of all my executive's emails, I can easily re-route emails to other members of the team to handle. But of course you also need to be sensitive about how you manage this and I found that building personal relationships is absolutely vital to people understanding if you inadvertently offend someone by forwarding their request to someone other than the chief executive, particularly if they are used to dealing with him directly. (JP & IA)

Managing access

When effectively managed, the executive's calendar is an accurate reflection of time commitments. When urgent matters arise it is your role as 'gate-keeper' to ascertain if an intervention is necessary and how best to achieve the outcome with minimum disruption. In my experience, EAs are in a pivotal position so consulting the EA regarding the executive's availability is always the most efficient avenue to facilitate access.

As the first point of contact it is the EA's responsibility to gather information pertaining to any request that arises and evaluate based on urgency and specific circumstances. The EA may also need to be quite assertive when making the assessment; and in many cases may defer/refer to another director as appropriate. An established EA acts as a conduit between the executive and the director team, so can confidently assist and resolve these types of situations.

When receiving and evaluating an inquiry or request, either internally or externally, the EA's judgement and investigative skills are essential. In my recent experiences, external callers (marketers especially) are very cunning and like to imply they already have a connection with the executive. So you need to be extremely thorough in your inquiry to make an assessment and resolve accordingly. Internally, it is my responsibility to limit the executive's involvement in 'hygiene' matters, and where possible redirect. (HC)

Part of my role is having to be mindful of others seeking EA knowledge and/or sharing gossip. My stance is always that I am unable to comment: if someone has an issue they should raise it with their manager or email my executive and offer a solution. I always ask others seeking a meeting for more detail so I am across the urgency of the matter – the subject, bullet points outlining the detail or a paper they can attach, and the urgency. Often I find it can wait a week or so rather than needing to be the next day. (MJ)

No doubt every EA has to deal with this, but it is difficult to manage people's expectations when it comes to getting access to the executive's time. Therefore it's really important to understand why the person in question needs time from the executive in the first place. Their issue or question might seem unimportant to the EA or executive, but it might also be preventing further work being done by the person making the request. It could have knock-on implications around the business which are not initially obvious. So it's very important to fully understand their issue or question before sending them away. A great executive will want to prioritise their time for the good of the business, so if they understand that delaying an otherwise important meeting by five minutes can give someone the decision they need to carry on with their project, then no doubt they will want to do this. (YP)

I was fortunate enough to partner with a very successful up and coming CEO. Cultured, intelligent, humble, funny, and wait for it … emotionally intelligent. (Yes, emotionally intelligent CEOs do exist!) Amazing as he was, these wonderful traits were also working to his disadvantage. He was extremely generous with his time, always happy to support his immediate team and anyone else who requested it. This came at a cost. Without a door on his office and with no one to stem the flow of visitors, the constant interruptions made it difficult for him to be most effective in his role.

Our first chat about how to best manage this was met with resistance, not because he didn't want my help but because he didn't want to shut anyone out. In short, I asked him to trust me, promised him I wouldn't destroy any relationships, would give everyone time with him and in the process, make him more effective. At this point in time, he still barely knew me but trusted his instinct enough to let me try.

Patterns are hard to change, especially when they involve headstrong people used to getting their own way. If I say most of the team comprised of engineers, I think you know I had my work cut out for me.

Without a door on his office to help me divert the tide of visitors, I set about becoming very comfortable with uncomfortable conversations. I would walk out from behind my desk and greet people to start a conversation, only for them to try to walk straight past me. I would ask them to stop, which was followed by a look that said, 'Did she really just say no to me?' followed by a pause.

'I'm sorry, did you say something?' they would say.

Deep breath. 'Yes – do you have a moment?'

I would explain that the executive was is the middle of something at the moment and that I really wanted to give him a while to finish it. Could I call you when he's ready?

'Well, it was just going to take a moment,' they would say.

'Gosh, I can see that you really want to talk to him but I'm sure you can appreciate how hard it is to get back a train of thought when you're interrupted in the middle of something. Would you do me a favour? Give me 20 minutes. If you don't hear from me, come straight back and go in. Okay?'

When eventually going in to see the boss, who while enthusiastically typing away at his computer with the bliss of an uninterrupted 20 minutes had been listening the whole time. If he was done, I would go and get the person who had tried to visit.

Baby steps are important, and so was surviving those withering looks headed my way. The look on one engineer's face said it all and several weeks later he actually called me a dragon within earshot. But in reality, I think he thought of me as the troll under the bridge.

For any changes like this to be truly effective, you and your CEO need to back each other up. So when someone aired their displeasure at having to wait, my executive made it clear that we were on the same page. This helped.

By the end of the month, they all knew the dragon was there and boy was I unpopular. But at the same time they were all getting quality, uninterrupted time with the boss. By two months, distraction techniques had crept in: one engineer talking to me while another tried to enter the office from another direction, but they didn't win. By three months, 'dragon' was an affectionate term. 'Go see the dragon, she'll sort you out.' The engineers and I were forming solid relationships that ended up being more like family than any other office I'd known.

By the end of my tenure everyone had learned that if you wanted to get anything done you saw the dragon first. The CEO would pop his head and out and say hello, only to be told by them that they were there to see me. I knew how he ticked and what needed to be in place for meetings with him to be most effective.

It's important to note that I never spoke for him but I did have strong insights into the way he worked. I was able to guide people to the best outcomes. It was hard work but I'd do it all again in a heartbeat. It was the start of an amazing journey with an inspirational group of leaders and the source of many great anecdotes. (JW)

Protecting the executive from themselves

I provide my executive with a list of things that he needs to prioritise, I make sure his office is free of clutter so he has a clear space to concentrate, I offer him coffee and make sure he takes a lunch break to go outside and take a walk. I also stay back and offer conversation if I feel it may be needed after hours. (MJ)

Being an EA today means so much more than managing diaries, organising travel and helping with emails. You have to be a guardian and protector … Protecting the executive from themselves is one such example. I once worked for a CEO who wanted to add a 'happy dance' to a presentation that was to be given at an industry event the following week. She sent me a clip she wanted embedded and when I opened it, I gasped. She thought it was hip and modern but I thought it was inappropriate material. She did not see what I was seeing and it was risky given the public forum it was to be presented at. I suggested I find something else and we use her clip at the next staff meeting. Luckily, she had forgotten about it by then! (MLJ)

My executive is a very understated and considerate person. There are a number of topics he is particularly passionate about, which can make it challenging for him to bring a meeting to an end. It is my role to provide a polite reminder that he has another appointment to keep his schedule on track, which enables him to give appropriate levels of time to each area of the business and a sense of an open-door policy for all. (JP & IA)

It is important to be able to anticipate and take care of the executive's needs, often before the executive is aware of them, and to be proactive in initiating the completion of requested tasks. To do this, the EA needs to know their executive's style and have a good understanding of their areas of responsibility so that the EA can coordinate and deliver what the executive needs. (NJ)

There are times when your 'read' of a situation may require an intervention (coffee) or a polite reminder to your executive regarding timing or responding to a request, to enable the executive to maintain their focus and keep them on schedule. Discussing the top priorities for the day at the morning catch-up is essential for identifying and sharing what is to be achieved. Likewise reviewing the task list regularly to keep abreast of commitments and to identify opportunities to assist or delegate is also effective in 'keeping the focus'. Knowing the habits of your executive is essential to preempt their needs and for planning their schedule, whether it be coffee, food, time at the gym or time with family. (HC)

Corporate thermometer and glue

Most of the managers in our group are fairly self-sufficient and once given a task to complete they generally go on their way without any fuss. To assist them in doing that, I have developed a good relationship and connection with each of them. I offer my knowledge and talent and they appreciate me offering authentic views and opinions to perform as required to get their tasks done.

As an outsider with a bird's-eye view I can often detect and observe good and bad behaviour among the team. I like to get to the bottom of any issues, research and understand the contributing factors and come to a solution before it gets to 'crisis' level. It doesn't always happen, but I generally can feel a vibe when I need to help out or engage my manager. (MR)

[Acting as a corporate thermometer for my executive] is an everyday occurrence based on gossip that is overheard or elevator chat that I feed back to my executive. I also meet with other EAs to find out any information within their departments that may be useful to my executive. If there is some good or exciting news within our department I make sure my executive speaks to the person responsible face to face and acknowledges their great behaviour and the difference it makes. The power of fabulous feedback being acknowledged by your leader is amazing! (MJ)

Many executives have entered into their role without formal management training; their technical skills or knowledge got them their promotion. A good EA can help with the management side of their job, benefiting both the executive and the EA. EAs provide a unique opportunity for companies to find out the true performance of executives and to know how staff really feel about their work place. Staff feel less inhibited discussing with an EA what really affects them in the workplace, especially if it is about management or a project going wrong. EAs are also given insight, due to the nature of their job involving working with managers on behalf of their boss, into the performance of an executive's management team. The observations made by an EA are frequent and mostly go unnoticed, giving a more accurate view of behaviours and competencies. Using EA observations, both up and down the company hierarchy, can provide many benefits, including helping to pre-empt issues, effectively sorting out operational problems, reducing company compliance risks, and increasing the effectiveness of performance across all areas. Often management will hire a consulting agency to find out the reasons for a work-related problem. Who do you think the consultants liaise with in the first place to get information on what is wrong?

The EA is in a unique position to engage with all workers and management as well as key clientele. This provides free work culture observations when staff aren't happy or when a client-based issue is in the making. The EA's ability to engage with staff to mitigate issues which may otherwise not have reached management until it was too late is one of the key benefits of hiring and utilising a genuine EA. But this often goes unseen and unknown when the issue has been mitigated before it reaches management or the boss. Executive assistants use the operational processes of an organisation to complete the practical part of their work. There are no staff in a better position than an EA to accurately identify the flaws of a process and provide solutions. They also know how to effectively implement work practices, if given the opportunity. (LV)

At Cranbrook, Michelle was the one constant that kept our executive team going. As teachers, we were constantly passing each other in corridors between classes, sport and extra-curricular activities, but never really connecting. Michelle was always available, always approachable, kept us on an even keel and heading in the right direction. She was a conduit for information who intuitively knew who needed a kick and who needed a hug! (GE-A)

I once had an instance where someone on the executive team had spent a lot of time working on a specific project, and they had spoken to me about it in depth throughout. Another executive didn't really appreciate the work involved, nor the impact that his disinterest had been having on the teams involved. The first executive was getting very frustrated that his meetings with the second executive were constantly cancelled at short notice and he was starting to feel very dejected. I understood why the second executive wasn't very interested, but explained the situation to him and told him what impact his actions were having. I told him that he needed to make time to listen to the first executive, and make him feel as though his work was valuable. I could see that it was and so I wanted to make sure he had the enthusiasm to carry the project on to completion. I arranged for the first executive to take the second through the entire project and made certain that this meeting was not moved or cancelled. Ultimately, the project got finished, and the whole executive team agreed that it had been extremely valuable to the company. (YP)

An EA can also be more alert to the nuances of interpersonal relationships among staff than a busy chief executive would necessarily be. This knowledge can be invaluable when smoothing out the inevitable difficulties or misunderstandings that arise in a fast-moving company. (JP & IA)

Supporting initiatives

I try to support my executive's initiatives every day by being passionate, engaged, interested and involved. Change is constant so there is no sense ignoring it – it's exciting! I love the opportunity to drive change. Currently our project department has an 'ideas' room every Friday afternoon, where people are invited to drop by and join in the conversation, to share ideas and make some quick wins within the company. I decided to lead a tour of our department staff to the room, so they could see it. Some of our staff aren't that actively involved and I want to build the passion in them to see what we are doing as an organisation and to give them a voice. (MJ)

EAs hold influential positions and can provide leadership within their business by embracing change, actively demonstrating the benefits and sharing their knowledge. Often I am nominated to be part of project implementation as a super user. I find the best way to embrace change is to apply the new knowledge and share this with others. (HC)

I work with a group of people who generally fit into one of two categories: experienced and senior, or junior millennial. The attitudes to work are very different. The senior people have 'done their time' on lower level tasks, and often have a better understanding of the bigger picture of the company. The millennials see their friends and colleagues working with flexible hours, or working from home, and have been brought up in a world where everything is instant and on-demand. Sometimes I have to remind the executives that the working culture is changing, and people aren't going to work 14-hour days just because that used to be done. Newer employees these days want to see what impact their work is having on the company – they aren't going to just sit back and do repetitive tasks over and over again. Their culture is such that they will be thinking, 'There must be an app for this'. This is the type of feedback and insight I have been able to provide to my CEO and other senior managers that has had huge impacts on the growth of the organisation. (YP)

Networking

Building strong internal working relationships are important in the EAs role in order to facilitate outcomes. Providing guidance and offering assistance, is the pre-cursor to establishing trust and respect with internal reports and colleagues. In my role I am responsible for many project coordination assignments, where I need to work and rely on other EAs in the business to assist their Executives in completing a task. I find that providing guidance, clarifying expectations and giving ownership to the EAs assists me in achieving the outcome. (HC)

It is important to not only build relationships internally but also externally. Being active with external networking takes time and contribution – however these opportunities are also great avenues to build your profile and that of your business. For example, I have found that through participating in professional development activities such as networking, online groups and webinars, and external memberships, are all opportunities to represent and profile yourself and your business. Sharing your knowledge and establishing new contacts can often lead to great sources of referrals and business opportunities. (HC)

I always try to get involved in opportunities around the company where I can. It's a great way to network and meet new people within the business. I am always on the lookout for new ways of doing tasks that may be more efficient. I am an active member of our OHS, philanthropy and entertainment committees. I have active engagement with other departments and have played a role in process changes such as the travel policy, developed a new process for travel authorisation, initiated a communications email to our department and am also leading the way for an EA network internet site so our EAs can share ideas and information (something our company has never done within our EA group). (MJ)

I am always on good terms with external stakeholders. I have developed strong relationships with venue/catering businesses and now they engage with me on a regular basis to keep me across any new venue opportunities that may arise. I find it's very important to go to EA networking events, as you never know who you will meet and sharing information is vital in the EA world. (MJ)

I worked for an executive who couldn't get a meeting with a prospective client. As I am a member of the EAN, I found out who his EA was and invited her to a 'Business Chicks' breakfast. When I rang to request a meeting between my executive and this EA's boss following that event, I was able to get it. (MLJ)

Modern EAs need to appreciate the significance and importance of networking externally. I make a huge effort to network with other EAs, PAs, suppliers, and anyone else with whom I could speak about anything work related. Not only have I built relationships with recruitment companies who have ultimately been able to place exceptional candidates at heavily reduced fees, but I have made contacts at various suppliers who might ultimately be able to use our services. (YP)

Our thanks to the following contributors to this appendix, along with their executives:

Helen Croker (HC), Assistant to Chief Executive, Prosperity Advisers Group

Michelle Le Jeune (MLJ), executive assistant to (among others) John Palisi (JPa), CFO, Prime Media Group, and Genet Erickson-Adam (GE-A), Deputy Head - Curriculum P–6, Cranbrook School

Mandy Johnston (MJ), Executive Assistant, UniSuper

Natasha Jonoski (NJ)

Janice Parker (JP), Executive Assistant to Ismail Ahmed (IA), Founder and CEO, WorldRemit

Yvette Pearson (YP), Office Manager, ESF Capital

Maria Racovalis (MR), Executive Assistant to Bruce Moore (BM)

Linda Viscovic (LV), Executive Assistant

Jody Webb (JW)

About the author

Jonathan McIlroy always dreamed of writing a book. Up until a year ago he had envisaged it would be a novel, however this book is evidence that things didn't turn out that way.

This book evolved out of Jonathan's passion for business management and leadership, and in particular a passion for all things 'EA', from their working practices to education and development, their role structure to the relationships they have with their executives, and how all of these affect executive and business performance.

He sees *The New Executive Assistant* very much as a book he had to write, having been confronted on so many occasions with poor business practices, outdated EA position descriptions, dysfunctional EA-executive working relationships and many other indicators that organisations were failing to get the best possible results out of their EAs, and in turn the best possible outcomes for their executives and the broader organisation.

From harbouring early political ambitions to spending many years working directly in or on the periphery of the finance and investment industries, Jonathan held various junior then senior management positions before ultimately establishing Executive Assistant Network in 2005 with his business partner, Natasha Cannon. They both realised the need for more formalised support and education initiatives for EAs.

Having grown up in Northern Ireland, Jonathan attended university in Edinburgh, followed by stints in Washington DC and London, before he moved to Australia in 2001. He currently resides in the beautiful northern beaches area of Sydney and considers himself extremely blessed to call such an amazing part of Australia his home.

CPSIA information can be obtained
at www.ICGtesting.com
Printed in the USA
LVHW040959040820
662297LV00003B/171

9 780648 116301